SCOTT FORESMAN · ADDISON WESLEY

Mathematics

Grade 1

Practice Masters/Workbook

PEARSON

Scott Foresman

Editorial Offices: Glenview, Illinois • Parsippany, New Jersey • New York, New York

Sales Offices: Needham, Massachusetts • Duluth, Georgia • Glenview, Illinois
Coppell, Texas • Ontario, California • Mesa, Arizona

Overview

Practice Masters/Workbook provides additional practice on the concept or concepts taught in each lesson.

ISBN 0-328-11681-5

10 V084 09

Making 6

We can show 6 in different ways.
Write the numbers that show ways to make 6.

1.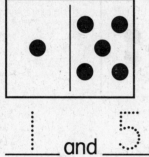

   __1__ and __5__

2.

   _____ and _____

3.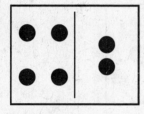

   _____ and _____

4.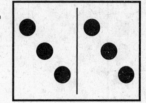

   _____ and _____

5.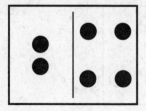

   _____ and _____

6.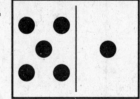

   _____ and _____

Problem Solving *Reasoning*

Solve.

7. Bernie has 3 cats and 2 dogs.
   How many pets does he have in all?

   _____

Making 7

We can show 7 in different ways.
Write the numbers that show ways to make 7.

I.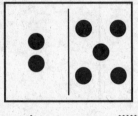

__2__ and __5__

2.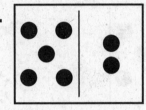

_____ and _____

3.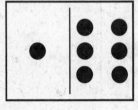

_____ and _____

4.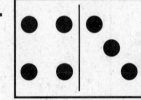

_____ and _____

5.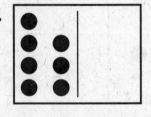

_____ and _____

6.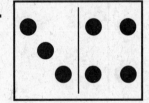

_____ and _____

Problem Solving *Number Sense*

Circle **yes** or **no**.

7. Jill has 5 dots. Can she put the
   same number of dots on each hat?

yes   no

Making 8 and 9

We can show 8 and 9 in different ways.

Write the numbers that show ways to make 8 and 9.

I.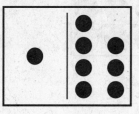

_4_ and _4_

2.

_____ and _____

3.

_____ and _____

4.

_____ and _____

5.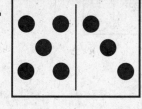

_____ and _____

6.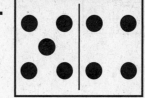

_____ and _____

Problem Solving *Visual Thinking*

7. Write the numbers to match the picture.

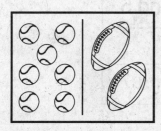

_____ and _____

Making 10

We can show 10 in different ways.

Write the numbers that show ways to make 10.

1.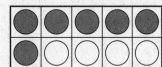

_8_ and _2_

2.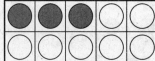

_____ and _____

3.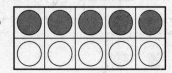

_____ and _____

4.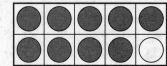

_____ and _____

5.

_____ and _____

6.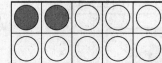

_____ and _____

Problem Solving *Number Sense*

7. Circle all the ways that make 10.

| 4 and 5 | 3 and 7 | 5 and 5 |

| 8 and 2 | 6 and 3 | 2 and 7 |

PROBLEM-SOLVING STRATEGY

Use Objects

In what different ways can you put 6 balls into 2 boxes?
Complete the chart.

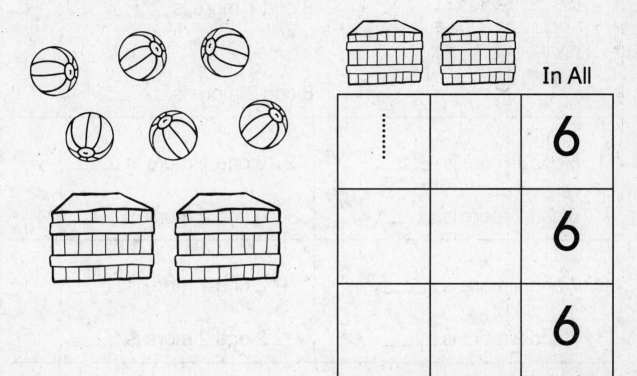

		In All
⋮		**6**
		6
		6

Reasoning *Writing in Math*

Write your own question about
putting some balls into 2 boxes.

_____

_____

_____

Name _____

1 and 2 More Than

Write the numbers.

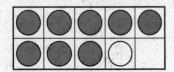

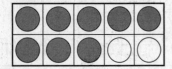

8 and 1 more is __9__.

8 and 2 more is _____.

---

1. 5 and 1 more is _____.

5 and 2 more is _____.

2. 0 and 1 more is _____.

0 and 2 more is _____.

---

3. 7 and 1 more is _____.

7 and 2 more is _____.

4. 2 and 1 more is _____.

2 and 2 more is _____.

Problem Solving *Algebra*

Write the numbers.

5. 4 and _____ more is 5.

4 and _____ more is 6.

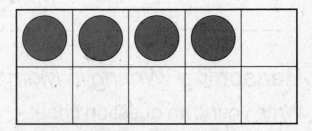

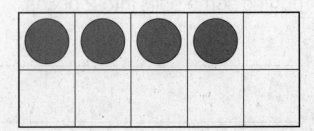

I and 2 Fewer Than

Write the numbers.

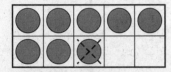

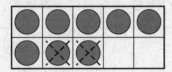

I fewer than 8 is __7__.

2 fewer than 8 is _____.

I. I fewer than 5 is _____. 2 fewer than 5 is _____.	**2.** I fewer than 10 is _____. 2 fewer than 10 is _____.
3. I fewer than 2 is _____. 2 fewer than 2 is _____.	**4.** I fewer than 11 is _____. 2 fewer than 11 is _____.

Problem Solving *Algebra*

Write the numbers.

5. I fewer than _____ is 8.

2 fewer than _____ is 7.

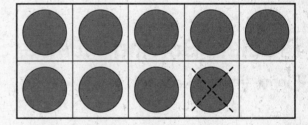

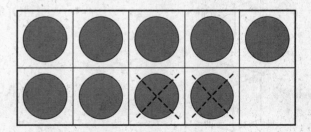

Comparing Numbers to 5 and to 10

Circle **fewer** or **more**.

1.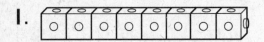

   8 is _____ than 10. (fewer)   more

2.

   2 is _____ than 5.   fewer   more

3.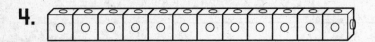

   7 is _____ than 5.   fewer   more

4.

   12 is _____ than 10.   fewer   more

Problem Solving *Number Sense*

Draw lines to match.

5.   more than 5

             more than 10

             fewer than 5

Ordering Numbers Through 12

Write the numbers in order from least to greatest.

1.

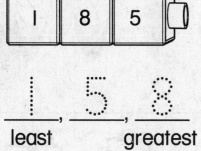

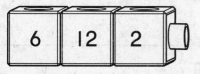

$\underline{}$, $\underline{}$, $\underline{}$
least   greatest

2.

6   12   2

_____, _____, _____
least   greatest

3.

7   5   10

_____, _____, _____
least   greatest

4.

4   1   2

_____, _____, _____
least   greatest

5.

8   12   10

_____, _____, _____
least   greatest

Problem Solving *Reasoning*

6. Kate, Jake, and Matt walk to school.

   Kate walks 5 blocks.

   Jake walks 3 blocks.

   Matt walks 6 blocks.

   Who walks the least blocks? _____

Identifying the Pattern Unit

Circle the pattern unit.

1.

2.

3.

4.

Problem Solving *Algebra*

Circle the shape that does **not** belong in the pattern.

5.

Translating Patterns

Look at the pattern.
Make the same pattern using letters.

1.

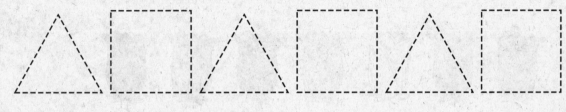

A   B   A   B   A   B

2.

A   B   C

Problem Solving *Reasoning*

3. Look at the pattern.
   Make the same pattern using letters.

1 2 2 1 2 2 1 2 2

A   B   B

Use Data from a Picture

Find the pattern.
Color what is missing.

1.

2.

3.

Problem Solving *Visual Thinking*

4. Find the pattern.
   Color what is missing.

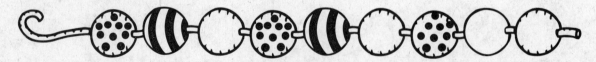

Name _____

It's a Party!

1. Manuel and Dee are setting the table for a party.
   Draw what comes next in the pattern.

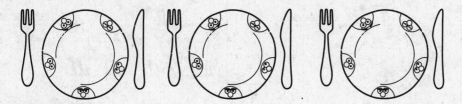

_____

2. Manuel hangs up 9 party lights. If he hangs up
   2 more party lights, how many party lights will
   be hanging up?   _____ lights

3. There are 7 chairs at the table. How many chairs
   will there be if 2 more are brought to the table?   _____ chairs

Writing in Math

4. Draw 6 children playing a game.
   Color some of their shirts blue and some
   of their shirts yellow to show 2 teams.
   Then finish the sentence.

   _____ and _____

Name _____

Stories About Joining

Use counters to answer each question.

1.

4 sheep are in the grass.

4 sheep join them.

How many sheep are there in all? ☐ sheep

2.

6 ducks are swimming.

3 ducks join them.

How many ducks are there in all? ☐ ducks

Problem Solving *Writing in Math*

3. Draw a picture of 4 blue
balloons and 3 red balloons.
Tell how many balloons there are in all.

_____ balloons

Name _____

Using Counters to Add

Add to find the sum.
Use counters if you like.

1.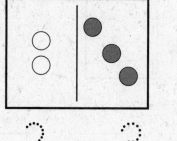

____2____ and ____3____ is ____5____ .

2.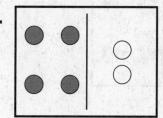

_____ and _____ is _____ .

3.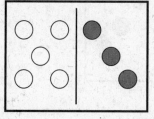

_____ and _____ is _____ .

4.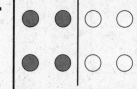

_____ and _____ is _____ .

5.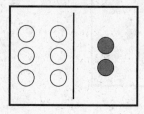

_____ and _____ is _____ .

6.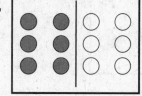

_____ and _____ is _____ .

Problem Solving *Reasoning*

7. Is the sum of 3 and 3 more or less than 7? _____

Using Numbers to Add

Write an addition sentence.

1.

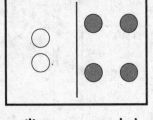

$$\underline{2} + \underline{4} = \underline{6}$$

2.

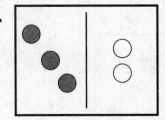

___ + ___ = ___

3.

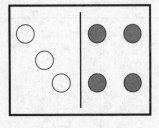

___ + ___ = ___

4.

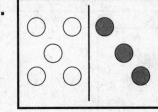

___ + ___ = ___

5.

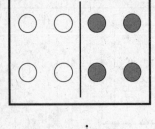

___ + ___ = ___

6.

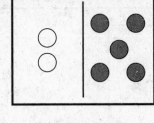

___ + ___ = ___

Problem Solving *Algebra*

7. Ron has 8 caps.

4 of his caps are blue.

The rest of his caps are red.

How many of Ron's caps are red?

_____ red caps

Name _____

Zero in Addition

Write an addition sentence.

1.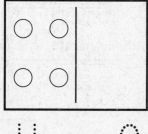

$$4 + 0 = 4$$

2.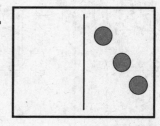

___ + ___ = ___

3.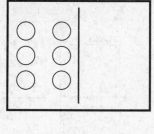

___ + ___ = ___

4.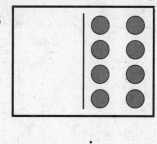

___ + ___ = ___

5.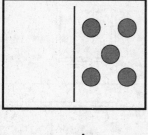

___ + ___ = ___

6.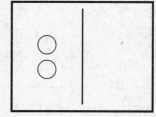

___ + ___ = ___

Problem Solving *Mental Math*

7. You see 2 nests in the tree.
   You see 4 baby birds in one nest.
   You see none in the other nest.
   How many baby birds do you see?

_____ baby birds

Vertical Addition

Add to find the sum.

1.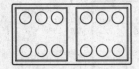

6 + 6 = __12__

$$\begin{array}{r} 6 \\ +\ 6 \\ \hline 12 \end{array}$$

2.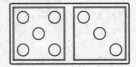

5 + 3 = _____

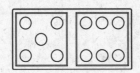
$$\begin{array}{r} 5 \\ +\ 3 \\ \hline \end{array}$$

3.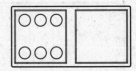

6 + 0 = _____

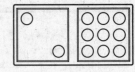
$$\begin{array}{r} 6 \\ +\ 0 \\ \hline \end{array}$$

4.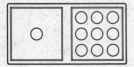

1 + 9 = _____

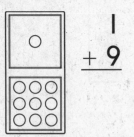
$$\begin{array}{r} 1 \\ +\ 9 \\ \hline \end{array}$$

5.

5 + 6 = _____

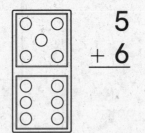
$$\begin{array}{r} 5 \\ +\ 6 \\ \hline \end{array}$$

6.

2 + 9 = _____

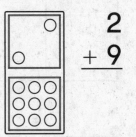
$$\begin{array}{r} 2 \\ +\ 9 \\ \hline \end{array}$$

Problem Solving *Number Sense*

7. Complete the pattern.

$$\begin{array}{r} 2 \\ +\ 2 \\ \hline 4 \end{array} \qquad \begin{array}{r} 3 \\ +\ 2 \\ \hline 5 \end{array} \qquad \begin{array}{r} 4 \\ +\ 2 \\ \hline 6 \end{array} \qquad \begin{array}{r} 5 \\ +\ 2 \\ \hline \boxed{} \end{array}$$

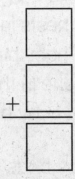

PROBLEM-SOLVING STRATEGY

Write A Number Sentence

Write an addition sentence to answer the question.

1. There are 4 rabbits in the garden.
5 more rabbits come.
How many rabbits
are there in all?

$$\underline{4} + \underline{5} = \underline{9}$$

2. There are 6 squirrels in the tree.
5 more squirrels are on the ground.
How many squirrels are there in all?

$$\underline{} + \underline{} = \underline{}$$

3. Jane finds 8 shells.
She finds 4 more shells.
How many shells does
Jane have in all?

$$\underline{} + \underline{} = \underline{}$$

4. There are 7 apples on the table.
Tim puts 3 more apples on the table.
How many apples are on the table?

$$\underline{} + \underline{} = \underline{}$$

Stories About Separating

Use counters to answer each question.

1.

There are 5 children at the table.

3 children are eating.

How many children are not eating? ▢ children

2.

A man has 7 balloons.

2 balloons fly away.

How many balloons does the man have now? ▢ balloons

Problem Solving *Number Sense*

3. Use counters to answer the question.

   There are 6 fish.

   2 swim away.

   How many fish did not swim away? ▢ fish

Using Counters to Subtract

Subtract to find the difference.
Use counters if you like.

1.

____4____ take away ____2____ is ____2____.

2.

_____ take away _____ is _____.

3.

_____ take away _____ is _____.

4.

_____ take away _____ is _____.

5.

_____ take away _____ is _____.

6.

_____ take away _____ is _____.

Problem Solving *Number Sense*

7. What is the most you can
   take away from 5 counters?
   Draw a picture to show
   that number.

Using Numbers to Subtract

Write a subtraction sentence.

1.

$$6 - 2 = 4$$

2.

___ ___ ___

3.

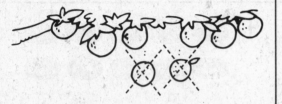

___ ___ ___

4.

___ ___ ___

5.

___ ___ ___

6.

___ ___ ___

Problem Solving *Writing in Math*

7. Draw a picture that shows
subtraction. Write a
subtraction sentence to
go with it.

_____

Zero in Subtraction

Write a subtraction sentence.

1.

$$5 - 5 = 0$$

2.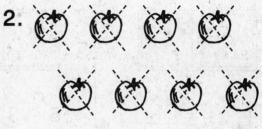

____ ____ = ____

3.

____ ____ = ____

4.

____ ____ = ____

5.

Purple Orange Brown Black White

____ ____ = ____

6.

____ ____ = ____

Problem Solving *Mental Math*

7. If $4 - 0 = 4$, then what is $40 - 0$? _____

8. If $4 - 4 = 0$, then what is $40 - 40$? _____

Vertical Subtraction

Subtract to find the difference.

1.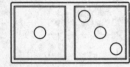

$4 - 1 = \underline{3}$

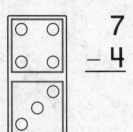

$$\begin{array}{r} 4 \\ -\ 1 \\ \hline 3 \end{array}$$

2.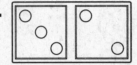

$5 - 3 = \underline{\quad}$

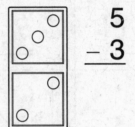

$$\begin{array}{r} 5 \\ -\ 3 \\ \hline \end{array}$$

3.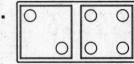

$6 - 2 = \underline{\quad}$

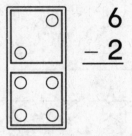

$$\begin{array}{r} 6 \\ -\ 2 \\ \hline \end{array}$$

4.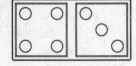

$7 - 4 = \underline{\quad}$

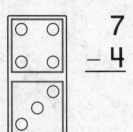

$$\begin{array}{r} 7 \\ -\ 4 \\ \hline \end{array}$$

5.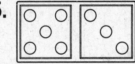

$8 - 5 = \underline{\quad}$

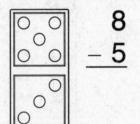

$$\begin{array}{r} 8 \\ -\ 5 \\ \hline \end{array}$$

6.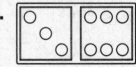

$9 - 3 = \underline{\quad}$

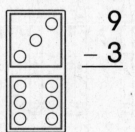

$$\begin{array}{r} 9 \\ -\ 3 \\ \hline \end{array}$$

Problem Solving *Visual Thinking*

Use the dominos to fill in the missing numbers.

7.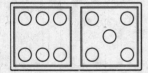

$11 - \boxed{} = 5$

8.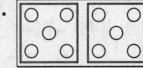

$\boxed{} - 5 = 5$

PROBLEM-SOLVING SKILL

Choose an Operation

Use the picture. Choose **add** or **subtract**.
Write the answer.

---

1. There are 5 ducks in the pond.
2 ducks fly away.
How many ducks did not fly away?   add   subtract

_____ ducks

---

2. 3 frogs are playing.
1 frog hops away.
How many frogs did not hop away?   add   subtract

_____ frogs

---

3. 2 turtles go for a swim.
4 more turtles sit on a rock.
How many turtles are there in all?   add   subtract

_____ turtles

Using Cubes to Compare

Write how many white cubes and how many gray cubes.

Then write how many more or how many fewer.

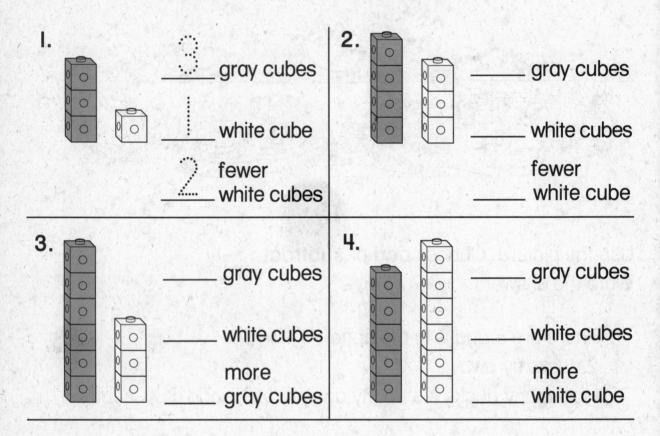

1.

_3_ gray cubes

_1_ white cube

_2_ fewer white cubes

2.

_____ gray cubes

_____ white cubes

_____ fewer white cube

3.

_____ gray cubes

_____ white cubes

_____ more gray cubes

4.

_____ gray cubes

_____ white cubes

_____ more white cube

Problem Solving *Visual Thinking*

5. Draw a picture to solve.

Dan has 5 model cars.

Tom has 3 model cars.

How many fewer model

cars does Tom have

than Dan?

_____ fewer model cars

Name _____

Using Subtraction to Compare

Write a subtraction sentence.
Then write how many more or how many fewer.

1. How many fewer dogs than bones?

____ ◯ ____ ◉ ____   ____ fewer dogs

2. How many more shoes than socks?

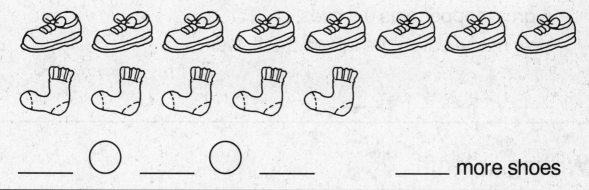

____ ◯ ____ ◯ ____   ____ more shoes

Problem Solving *Estimation*

Answer each question.

3. Does your class have more
boys or more girls?

more _____

4. Does your classroom have
fewer children or desks?

fewer _____

Name _____

Bugs, Bugs, Everywhere!

1. 4 crickets are chirping.
   3 more crickets begin chirping.
   How many crickets are chirping now?

   4 and 3 more is _____.

2. There are 9 flowers.
   There are 7 bees.
   How many fewer bees are there?

   _____ fewer than 9

3. There are 7 leaves on the flower.
   A grasshopper eats 0 leaves.
   How many leaves are left on the flower?

   _____ – _____ = _____

Writing in Math

4. Write an addition sentence or a subtraction sentence.

   _____ ◯ _____ ◯ _____

   Write a story about
   your number sentence.
   Then draw a picture.

Counting On 1, 2, or 3

Count on to solve. Use counters if you like.

1.

$$5 + 2 = \underline{}$$

2.

$$7 + 1 = \underline{}$$

3.

$$6 + 3 = \underline{}$$

4.

$$8 + 2 = \underline{}$$

5.

$$9 + 3 = \underline{}$$

6.

$$6 + 1 = \underline{}$$

Problem Solving *Number Sense*

Count on to solve.

7. Pam picks 5 flowers.
Then she picks 3 more.
How many flowers does
Pam have in all?

_____ flowers

8. Sal has 7 marbles.
He finds 2 more.
How many marbles
does Sal have now?

_____ marbles

Adding in Any Order

Add. Then write an addition sentence with the
addends in a different order.

1.

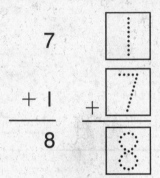

7	9	6
+ 1	+ 2	+ 0
8		

2.

4	6	5
+ 3	+ 4	+ 2

3. $8 + 3 =$ _____ $5 + 4 =$ _____ $6 + 3 =$ _____

___ + ___ = ___   ___ + ___ = ___   ___ + ___ = ___

Problem Solving *Visual Thinking*

4. Write two addition sentences
that tell about the picture.

___ + ___ = ___

___ + ___ = ___

 8 marbles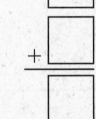

Adding 1, 2, or 3

Circle the greater number.
Then count on to add.

1. $(7) + 2 =$ ___9___ $1 + 5 =$ _____ $4 + 3 =$ _____

2. $10 + 2 =$ _____ $3 + 8 =$ _____ $6 + 3 =$ _____

3. $2 + 8 =$ _____ $1 + 7 =$ _____ $2 + 9 =$ _____

4.
$$
\begin{array}{cccccc}
2 & 5 & 8 & 11 & 3 & 10 \\
+3 & +2 & +3 & +1 & +7 & +1 \\
\end{array}
$$

5.
$$
\begin{array}{cccccc}
3 & 9 & 2 & 3 & 6 & 3 \\
+1 & +1 & +4 & +8 & +2 & +9 \\
\end{array}
$$

Problem Solving *Algebra*

Finish the picture and complete
the addition sentence.

6.

$5 + $ _____ $= 6$

7.

$3 + $ _____ $= 5$

Adding Using a Number Line

Add 1, 2, or 3. Use the number line to help you.

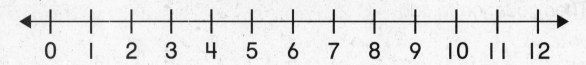

$$0 \quad 1 \quad 2 \quad 3 \quad 4 \quad 5 \quad 6 \quad 7 \quad 8 \quad 9 \quad 10 \quad 11 \quad 12$$

1.
$$\begin{array}{c} 7 \\ + 2 \\ \hline 9 \end{array} \qquad \begin{array}{c} 6 \\ + 1 \\ \hline \end{array} \qquad \begin{array}{c} 4 \\ + 2 \\ \hline \end{array} \qquad \begin{array}{c} 5 \\ + 2 \\ \hline \end{array} \qquad \begin{array}{c} 8 \\ + 1 \\ \hline \end{array} \qquad \begin{array}{c} 1 \\ + 7 \\ \hline \end{array}$$

2.
$$\begin{array}{c} 3 \\ + 1 \\ \hline \end{array} \qquad \begin{array}{c} 9 \\ + 2 \\ \hline \end{array} \qquad \begin{array}{c} 1 \\ + 4 \\ \hline \end{array} \qquad \begin{array}{c} 6 \\ + 2 \\ \hline \end{array} \qquad \begin{array}{c} 5 \\ + 3 \\ \hline \end{array} \qquad \begin{array}{c} 2 \\ + 8 \\ \hline \end{array}$$

3.
$$\begin{array}{c} 2 \\ + 10 \\ \hline \end{array} \qquad \begin{array}{c} 7 \\ + 3 \\ \hline \end{array} \qquad \begin{array}{c} 3 \\ + 6 \\ \hline \end{array} \qquad \begin{array}{c} 8 \\ + 3 \\ \hline \end{array} \qquad \begin{array}{c} 9 \\ + 3 \\ \hline \end{array} \qquad \begin{array}{c} 1 \\ + 11 \\ \hline \end{array}$$

Problem Solving *Writing in Math*

4. Draw to show the addition on the number line.
Then write the sum.

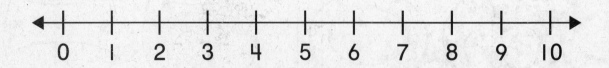

$$0 \quad 1 \quad 2 \quad 3 \quad 4 \quad 5 \quad 6 \quad 7 \quad 8 \quad 9 \quad 10$$

$2 + 6 = $ _____

Name _____

Extra Information

Cross out the extra information you do not need.
Then write a number sentence to solve the problem.

1. ~~Jane has 8 brown hamsters.~~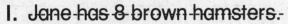
   She has 4 black dogs.
   She has 2 tan dogs.
   How many dogs does Jane have?

   $\underline{4}$ + $\underline{2}$ = $\underline{6}$ dogs

---

2. Dan gets 2 books.
   He reads 8 pages.
   The next day Dan gets
   2 more books.
   How many books did Dan get?

   _____ + _____ = _____ books

---

3. 4 frogs are on a lily pad.
   Billy wants a pet frog.
   6 frogs are on a rock.
   How many frogs are there?

   _____ + _____ = _____ frogs

---

4. 5 girls are playing jump rope.
   3 more girls are watching.
   2 boys are playing baseball.
   How many girls are there?

   _____ + _____ = _____ girls

Doubles

Circle the doubles. Then add.

1.
7	4	2	6	1	3
+ 1	+ 4	+ 5	+ 6	+ 1	+ 4
	8				

2.
4	3	7	2	9	5
+ 3	+ 3	+ 3	+ 8	+ 1	+ 5

3.
0	5	6	10	2	8
+ 0	+ 3	+ 2	+ 1	+ 2	+ 0

4. 9 + 3 = _____   6 + 6 = _____   3 + 6 = _____

5. 5 + 5 = _____   8 + 2 = _____   7 + 2 = _____

Problem Solving *Visual Thinking*

Write a number sentence to answer each question.

6.

How many balls are there in all?

_____ + _____ = _____

7.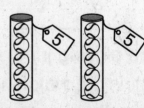

How many balls are there in all?

_____ + _____ = _____

Name _____

Doubles Plus I

Find each sum.
Use cubes if you like.

1.
   2   3   3   4   6   5
  + 2   + 2   + 4   + 4   + 5   + 5
  ---- ---- ---- ---- ---- ----
   4

2.
   4   2   0   1   3   1
  + 5   + 3   + 0   + 0   + 2   + 2
  ---- ---- ---- ---- ---- ----

3.
   1   5   5   6   3   4
  + 1   + 4   + 6   + 6   + 3   + 3
  ---- ---- ---- ---- ---- ----

Problem Solving *Algebra*

Write a double or a double plus one for each sum.

4.

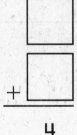
4

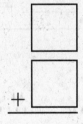
5

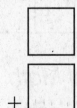
6

7

8

Sums of 10

Fill in the missing numbers to find a sum of 10.
Use ten-frames and counters if you like.

1.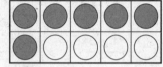

6

$+$

$6 + \underline{} = \underline{10}$

10

2.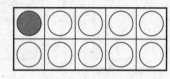

1

$+$

$1 + \underline{} = 10$

10

3.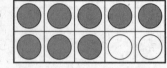

8

$+$

$8 + \underline{} = 10$

10

4.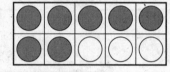

7

$+$

$7 + \underline{} = 10$

10

5.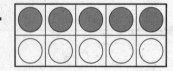

5

$+$

$5 + \underline{} = 10$

10

6.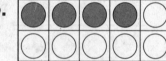

4

$+$

$4 + \underline{} = 10$

10

Problem Solving *Mental Math*

Circle the card that shows your answer.

7. Beth has 2 stickers.
How many more stickers
does she need to have
10 stickers?

 6 7 8

Name _____

Draw a Picture

Draw a picture. Then write a number sentence.

1. Dean has 6 stamps.
He gets 5 more stamps.
How many stamps does
he have in all?

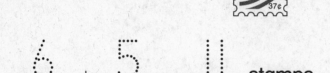

$\underline{6} + \underline{5} = \underline{11}$ stamps

---

2. Jan picks 8 red apples.
She picks 4 yellow apples.
How many apples does
Jan pick in all?

_____ + _____ = _____ apples

---

3. Jo Jo has 4 seashells in her pail.
She puts 5 more seashells into
the pail. How many seashells
are in her pail now?

_____ + _____ = _____ seashells

Name _____

Hop to It!

1. 10 rabbits hop into the garden.

   6 of them eat lettuce.

   The rest eat clover.

   How many eat clover?

   6 + _____ = 10

---

2. Kate has 1 cat and 1 bird.

   She has 1 gray rabbit.

   She has 2 white rabbits.

   How many rabbits does Kate have?

   _____ + _____ = _____ rabbits

---

3. 5 rabbits live in the backyard.

   6 more rabbits come to live with them.

   How many rabbits live in the backyard in all?

   There are _____ rabbits in all.

Writing in Math

4. Draw a picture to show
   8 rabbits in two groups.
   Write an addition sentence for your picture.

Counting Back Using a Number Line

Count back to subtract.
Use a number line if you like.

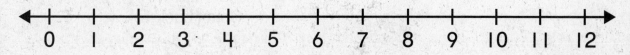

1.

6	4	7	3	4	5
− 2	− 1	− 1	− 2	− 2	− 1
4					

2.

7	6	5	3	8	9
− 2	− 1	− 2	− 1	− 2	− 1

3.

10	9	2	12	12	11
− 1	− 2	− 2	− 1	− 2	− 2

Problem Solving *Number Sense*

Use the number line to subtract.
Write the missing numbers. Look for a pattern.

4.

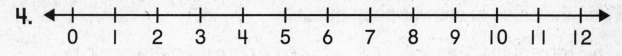

3	4	5	☐	7	☐
− ☐	− 2	− ☐	− 2	− 2	− 2
1	☐	3	4	☐	6

Name _____

Counting Back

Count back to subtract.
Use counters if you like.

1.  $\begin{array}{r} 7 \\ -\ 1 \\ \hline 6 \end{array}$

Start at 7.
Count back 1.

2. $\begin{array}{r} 11 \\ -\ 2 \\ \hline \end{array}$ $\begin{array}{r} 6 \\ -\ 1 \\ \hline \end{array}$ $\begin{array}{r} 1 \\ -\ 1 \\ \hline \end{array}$ $\begin{array}{r} 7 \\ -\ 1 \\ \hline \end{array}$ $\begin{array}{r} 3 \\ -\ 2 \\ \hline \end{array}$ $\begin{array}{r} 12 \\ -\ 1 \\ \hline \end{array}$

3. $\begin{array}{r} 5 \\ -\ 1 \\ \hline \end{array}$ $\begin{array}{r} 10 \\ -\ 2 \\ \hline \end{array}$ $\begin{array}{r} 9 \\ -\ 1 \\ \hline \end{array}$ $\begin{array}{r} 3 \\ -\ 1 \\ \hline \end{array}$ $\begin{array}{r} 6 \\ -\ 2 \\ \hline \end{array}$ $\begin{array}{r} 10 \\ -\ 1 \\ \hline \end{array}$

4. $\begin{array}{r} 2 \\ -\ 1 \\ \hline \end{array}$ $\begin{array}{r} 4 \\ -\ 2 \\ \hline \end{array}$ $\begin{array}{r} 12 \\ -\ 2 \\ \hline \end{array}$ $\begin{array}{r} 8 \\ -\ 2 \\ \hline \end{array}$ $\begin{array}{r} 11 \\ -\ 1 \\ \hline \end{array}$ $\begin{array}{r} 9 \\ -\ 2 \\ \hline \end{array}$

Problem Solving *Number Sense*

Use the clues to answer each question.

5. Tao counted back 2.
His answer was 5.
On what number
did he start? _____

6. Adam counted back 1.
His answer was 11.
On what number
did he start? _____

Using Doubles to Subtract

Add the doubles.

Then use the doubles to help you subtract.

1.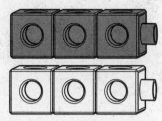

$$\begin{array}{r} 3 \\ + 3 \\ \hline 6 \end{array}$$

$$\begin{array}{r} 6 \\ - 3 \\ \hline 3 \end{array}$$

If $3 + 3 = 6$,
then $6 - 3 = 3$.

2.

$$\begin{array}{r} 4 \\ + 4 \\ \hline \end{array}$$

$$\begin{array}{r} 8 \\ - 4 \\ \hline \end{array}$$

3.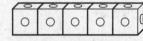

$$\begin{array}{r} 6 \\ + 6 \\ \hline \end{array}$$

$$\begin{array}{r} 12 \\ - 6 \\ \hline \end{array}$$

4.

$$\begin{array}{r} 2 \\ + 2 \\ \hline \end{array}$$

$$\begin{array}{r} 4 \\ - 2 \\ \hline \end{array}$$

5.

$$\begin{array}{r} 5 \\ + 5 \\ \hline \end{array}$$

$$\begin{array}{r} 10 \\ - 5 \\ \hline \end{array}$$

Problem Solving *Visual Thinking*

Write an addition sentence and a
subtraction sentence for the picture.

6.

____ + ____ = ____

____ − ____ = ____

PROBLEM-SOLVING STRATEGY　　　　　　　　　**P 4-4**

Write a Number Sentence

Write a subtraction sentence to answer each question.

1. Dana has 6 rings.
She gives 3 to Lyn.
How many rings does
Dana have left?

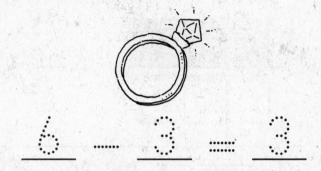

6 — 3 = 3

---

2. Ruth has 8 bananas
and 5 apples on a plate.
How many more bananas
does she have?

___ ___ ___

---

3. There are 9 cars and
4 trucks in the parking lot.
How many more cars
than trucks are there?

___ ___ ___

---

4. 10 birds are eating seeds.
5 birds fly away.
How many birds are left?

___ ___ ___

Name _____

Using Related Facts

Write an addition sentence and a subtraction
sentence for each picture.

1. ⬜⬜⬜
⬜⬜⬜⬜,⬜⬜⬜

$$\underline{3} + \underline{7} = \underline{10}$$

$$\underline{10} - \underline{3} = \underline{7}$$

> The first number in the
> subtraction sentence is
> the sum of the numbers
> in the addition sentence.

2. △△△△△△△△△
△

___ + ___ = ___

___ − ___ = ___

3. ☆☆
☆☆☆☆☆☆☆

___ + ___ = ___

___ − ___ = ___

4. ♡♡♡♡
♡♡♡♡♡

___ + ___ = ___

___ − ___ = ___

5. ◇◇◇◇◇◇◇◇
◇◇◇

___ + ___ = ___

___ − ___ = ___

Problem Solving *Writing in Math*

Draw a picture to show these related facts.

6. $6 + 3 = 9$ $\qquad\qquad 9 - 3 = 6$

Fact Families

Complete each fact family.
Use cubes if you like.

Most fact families
have 4 facts.

1.

$$\underline{3} + \underline{4} = \underline{7} \qquad \underline{7} - \underline{3} = \underline{4}$$

$$\underline{4} + \underline{3} = \underline{7} \qquad \underline{7} - \underline{4} = \underline{3}$$

2.

$$\underline{} + \underline{} = \underline{} \qquad \underline{} - \underline{} = \underline{}$$

$$\underline{} + \underline{} = \underline{} \qquad \underline{} - \underline{} = \underline{}$$

3.

$$\underline{} + \underline{} = \underline{} \qquad \underline{} - \underline{} = \underline{}$$

$$\underline{} + \underline{} = \underline{} \qquad \underline{} - \underline{} = \underline{}$$

Problem Solving *Algebra*

Write the missing signs to finish the fact family.

4. $8 \bigcirc 2 = 10 \qquad\qquad 10 \bigcirc 8 = 2$

$2 \bigcirc 8 = 10 \qquad\qquad 10 \bigcirc 2 = 8$

Name _____

Using Addition Facts to Subtract

Circle the addition fact that will help you subtract.
Then subtract.

1.
$9 - 4 = \underline{5}$

$(4 + 5 = 9)$
$6 + 2 = 8$

2.
$10 - 6 = \underline{\quad}$

$8 + 3 = 11$
$4 + 6 = 10$

3.
$11 - 8 = \underline{\quad}$

$5 + 2 = 7$
$8 + 3 = 11$

4.
$12 - 4 = \underline{\quad}$

$4 + 7 = 11$
$4 + 8 = 12$

5.
$5 - 3 = \underline{\quad}$

$3 + 2 = 5$
$5 + 1 = 6$

6.
$7 - 4 = \underline{\quad}$

$4 + 3 = 7$
$5 + 2 = 7$

Problem Solving *Mental Math*

7. May wants to read 9 pages in her book.
She reads 5 pages.
How many pages does
she have left to read?

_____ pages

PROBLEM-SOLVING SKILL

Choose an Operation

Circle **add** or **subtract**.
Then write a number sentence.

1. Tom made 6 bookmarks.
   He gave away 4 of them.
   How many bookmarks
   does Tom have left?

add   subtract

____ ◯ ____ = ____

---

2. There are 8 goldfish
   in the bowl. Tanya puts in
   1 more goldfish. How many
   goldfish are there now?

add   subtract

____ ◯ ____ = ____

---

3. There are 4 red apples and
   5 green apples. How many
   apples are there in all?

add   subtract

____ ◯ ____ = ____

---

4. There are 7 socks.
   Jan loses 3 of them.
   How many socks are left?

add   subtract

____ ◯ ____ = ____

Name _____

Playful Puppies

1. 8 puppies are playing. 5 puppies are sleeping.
How many more puppies are playing than sleeping?

_____ − _____ = _____

There are _____ more puppies playing.

2. 5 puppies are eating. 3 puppies join them.
How many puppies are eating now?

There are _____ puppies eating now.

3. There are 10 puppies in a basket. 5 puppies jump out.
How many puppies are left?

_____ − _____ = _____

4. Which doubles fact helped you solve Exercise 3?

_____ + _____ = _____

Writing in Math

5. Write an addition story about grown-up dogs.
Use pictures, numbers, or words.

Identifying Solid Figures

1. Color each solid figure below.

green   red   blue   yellow

2. Now put an X on each cube.

Problem Solving *Visual Thinking*

Finish drawing the rectangular prism.

3.

Flat Surfaces and Vertices

Circle the solid figure that answers each question.

1. Which solid figure has 2 flat surfaces and 0 vertices?

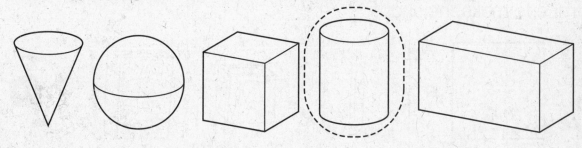

2. Which solid figure has 0 flat surfaces and 0 vertices?

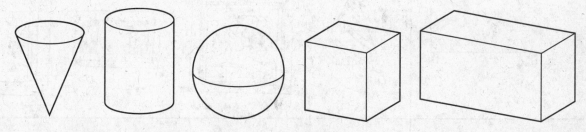

3. Which solid figures have 6 flat surfaces and 8 vertices?

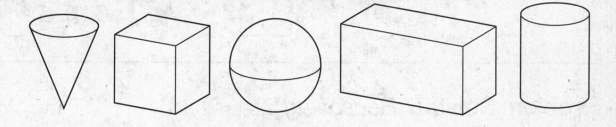

Problem Solving *Reasoning*

Use the clues to answer each question.

4. I have 1 flat surface.
   I have 0 vertices.
   Which solid figure am I?

   _____

5. I have 2 flat surfaces.
   I have no vertices.
   Which solid figure am I?

   _____

Relating Plane Shapes to Solid Figures

Look at the shape.
Then circle the objects you could
trace to make the shape.

1.

2.

3.

Problem Solving *Reasoning*

How are the two solid figures alike?
Circle each answer.

4.    same size   same shape

5.   same size   same shape

Name _____

Identifying Plane Shapes

I. Draw a rectangle.

2. Draw a square.

3. Draw a triangle.

4. Draw a circle.

Problem Solving *Algebra*

5. Draw the shape that comes next in the pattern.

Properties of Plane Shapes

1. Draw a shape with 4 vertices.

2. Draw a shape with fewer than 4 straight sides.

3. Draw a shape with more than 4 straight sides.

4. Draw a shape with more than 4 vertices.

Problem Solving *Reasonableness*

5. Here is the way that Brian sorted some plane shapes.

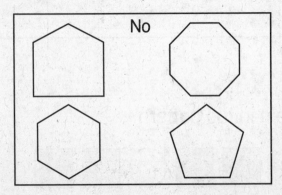

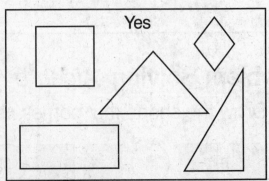

Circle the question that Brian might have asked.

Does it have fewer than 5 vertices?

Does it have more than 5 sides?

Same Size and Same Shape

Look at the first shape.
Then draw two shapes that match it.

1.
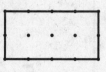

2.
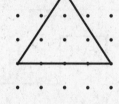

3.
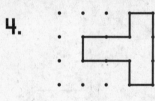

4.

Problem Solving *Visual Thinking*

5. Circle all of the squares.
   Then color the two squares that are
   the same size and the same shape.

Symmetry

Draw a **line of symmetry** to make two matching parts.

1.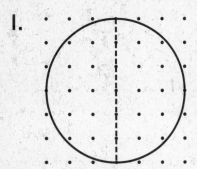

2.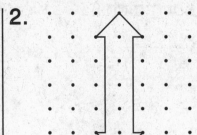

3.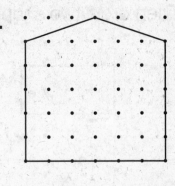

4.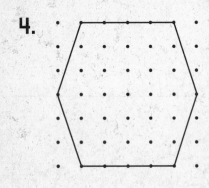

5.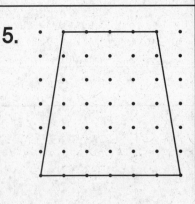

6.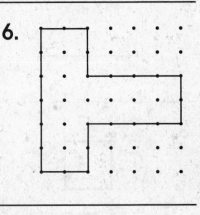

Problem Solving *Visual Thinking*

Draw a different line of symmetry on each shape.

7.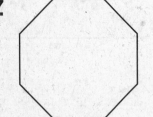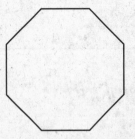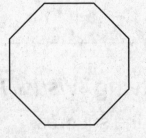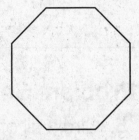

8.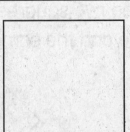

Slides, Flips, and Turns

Is it a **slide**, a **flip**, or a **turn**?
Circle the answer.

1.

slide   (flip)   turn

2.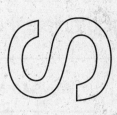

slide   flip   turn

3.

slide   flip   turn

4.

slide   flip   turn

Problem Solving *Visual Thinking*

5. Circle the shapes that will look the same
   after they are turned.

PROBLEM-SOLVING STRATEGY

Make an Organized List

1. Show 5 ways you can make
   this shape using pattern blocks.
   Complete the list.

Ways to Make △		
Shapes I Used ⬡	◇	△
Way 1	0	0	9
Way 2			
Way 3			
Way 4			
Way 5			

Writing in Math

2. How many ways can you use
   the pattern blocks to make a ◇? Explain.

_____

_____

_____

Equal Parts

Color the shapes that show equal parts.
Then write the number of equal parts
for all of the shapes.

1.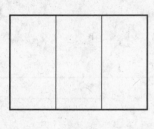

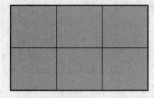

____

2.

____

3.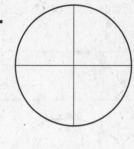

____

4.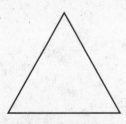

____

5.

____

6.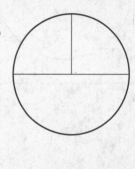

____

Problem Solving *Visual Thinking*

7. Draw straight lines to divide these shapes
into equal parts.

2 equal parts

4 equal parts

4 equal parts

Halves

Draw a straight line on each shape to show halves.

1. 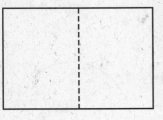	2. 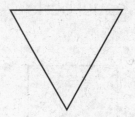	3. 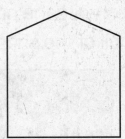
4. 	5. 	6. 
7. 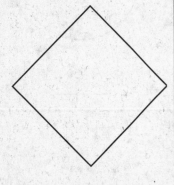	8.	9.

Problem Solving *Mental Math*

10. Ana, Alex, and Gwen want to share

1 orange. They cut the orange in half.

Will each child get $\frac{1}{2}$ of the orange? _____

Thirds and Fourths

Color 1 part of each shape.
Then circle the fraction.

1.

$\frac{1}{3}$ $\boxed{\frac{1}{4}}$

2.

$\frac{1}{3}$ $\frac{1}{4}$

3.

$\frac{1}{3}$ $\frac{1}{4}$

4.

$\frac{1}{3}$ $\frac{1}{4}$

5.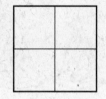

$\frac{1}{3}$ $\frac{1}{4}$

6.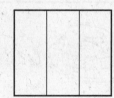

$\frac{1}{3}$ $\frac{1}{4}$

Problem Solving *Number Sense*

7. Jill ate $\frac{1}{3}$ of a pizza.

Mario ate $\frac{1}{4}$ of a pizza.

The pizzas are the same size.

Who ate more pizza?

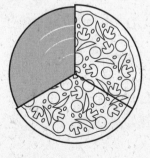

_____

Fractions of a Set

Color one object.
Then circle the fraction that tells what
part of the group you colored.

1.

$$\left(\frac{1}{2}\right) \qquad \frac{1}{3} \qquad \frac{1}{4}$$

2.

$$\frac{1}{2} \qquad \frac{1}{3} \qquad \frac{1}{4}$$

3.

$$\frac{1}{2} \qquad \frac{1}{3} \qquad \frac{1}{4}$$

4.

$$\frac{1}{2} \qquad \frac{1}{3} \qquad \frac{1}{4}$$

5.

$$\frac{1}{2} \qquad \frac{1}{3} \qquad \frac{1}{4}$$

6.

$$\frac{1}{2} \qquad \frac{1}{3} \qquad \frac{1}{4}$$

Problem Solving *Writing in Math*

7. Tim has a group of balloons.

$\frac{1}{3}$ of them are blue.

Draw Tim's balloons.

Non-Unit Fractions

Write the fraction that names the shaded part.

1.

2.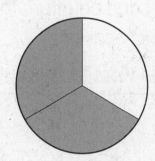

3.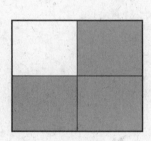

4.

5.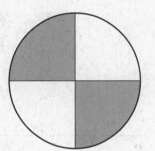

6.

Problem Solving *Number Sense*

7. Color to show $\frac{5}{8}$ on both.

   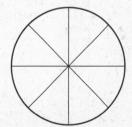

Use Data from a Chart

Use the chart and counters to solve.
Draw the equal shares.

Breakfast	
Eggs	12
Muffins	9
Pancakes	8

1. 4 children want to share the pancakes.

Each child gets ___2___ pancakes.

---

2. 3 children want to share the muffins.

Each child gets _____ muffins.

---

3. 6 children want to share the eggs.

Each child gets _____ eggs.

Name _____

Shapes All Around Us

1. Circle each cylinder.

2. Draw a box around each cone.

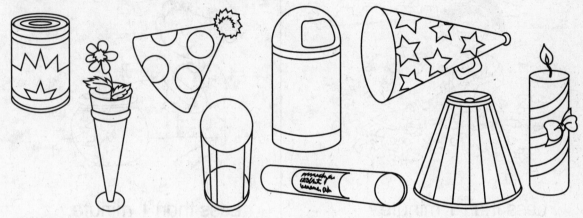

3. How many cylinders did you find? _____ cylinders

4. How many cones did you find? _____ cones

5. Write a number sentence to tell how many more
   cylinders there are than cones.

   _____ – _____ = _____ more cylinder.

Writing in Math

6. Count the cubes and spheres in your classroom.
   Draw a picture of each one of them that you find.
   Did you find more cubes or spheres? How many more?

Minutes

How long does each activity take?
Circle the correct answer.

1.

Less than I minute

(More than I minute)

2.

Less than I minute

More than I minute

3.

Less than I minute

More than I minute

4.

Less than I minute

More than I minute

Problem Solving *Estimation*

5. Draw a picture to show
   something that you can
   do in about the same time
   it takes to make your bed.

Understanding the Hour and Minute Hands

Draw an hour hand and a minute hand to show each time.

1.

7 o'clock

2.

10 o'clock

3.

2 o'clock

4.

1 o'clock

5.

8 o'clock

6.

11 o'clock

Problem Solving *Algebra*

Write the next two hours.

7. 4 o'clock _____ o'clock _____ o'clock

8. 8 o'clock _____ o'clock _____ o'clock

9. 1 o'clock _____ o'clock _____ o'clock

Telling and Writing Time to the Hour

Draw lines to match the clocks that
show the same time.

I.

3:00   4:00   9:00   2:00

2.

11:00   12:00   10:00   7:00

Problem Solving *Algebra*

Look for the pattern. Then write each missing time.

3. 12:00, 1:00, _____ : _____, 3:00, 4:00

4. 10:00, 11:00, _____ : _____, 1:00, 2:00

Telling and Writing Time to the Half Hour

Write the time shown on each clock.

1.

2.

3.

4.

5.

6.

Problem Solving *Visual Thinking*

7. Show 1 o'clock on the first clock.
   On the second clock show the time
   it will be in 30 minutes.

PROBLEM-SOLVING STRATEGY

Act It Out

Write the starting time and the ending time.
Draw hands on the clock to show the ending time.
Use a clock if you like.

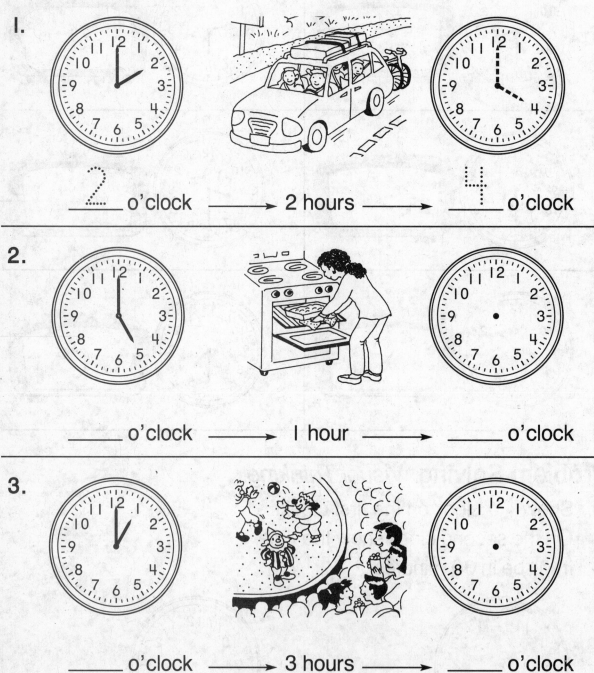

1.

_2_ o'clock ⟶ 2 hours ⟶ _4_ o'clock

2.

_____ o'clock ⟶ 1 hour ⟶ _____ o'clock

3.

_____ o'clock ⟶ 3 hours ⟶ _____ o'clock

Ordering Events

When did each of these things happen?
Draw lines to match.

1.

● morning   ● afternoon   ● night

2.

● morning   ● afternoon   ● night

Problem Solving *Writing in Math*

3. Draw a picture to show
something that you like to do.
Write **morning, afternoon,** or
night to match your picture.

Name _____

Estimating Lengths of Time

About how long does each activity take?
Draw lines to match.

I.

● about I minute   ● about I hour   ● about I day

2.

● about 2 minutes   ● about 2 hours   ● about 2 days

Problem Solving *Estimation*

3. Jake wants to be a basketball player. Should he practice shooting baskets each day for about I minute or about I hour?

4. Elaine wants to make a salad. Will she work for about 5 minutes or about 5 hours?

_____   _____

Name _____

Use Data from a Schedule

Use the schedule to answer the questions.

Day Camp Schedule		
Time	**Activity**	
9:00		Art
9:30		Tee-ball
10:00		Music
10:30		Puppet Theater
11:00		Swimming

1. What activity do the children do at 9:00? _____ _____

2. What activity do the children do just
   before music? _____

3. What activity do the children do just
   after puppet theater? _____

4. What time does music begin? _____

Problem Solving *Reasonableness*

5. The children are about to start music.
   Ned wants to know how long it is until
   it is time for swimming. Lou says it is
   about 1 hour. Is he correct? _____

Name _____

Days of the Week

1. Circle the names of the days of the week.

2. Color the Mondays blue and Wednesdays red.

April						
Sunday	Monday	Tuesday	Wednesday	Thursday	Friday	Saturday
	1	2	3	4	5	6
7	8	9	10	11	12	13
14	15	16	17	18	19	20
21	22	23	24	25	26	27
28	29	30				

3. Write the days of the week in order.

_____, Sunday _____ Monday _____, _____,

_____, _____, _____,

_____

Problem Solving *Visual Thinking*

Find the pattern. Then write the day that comes next.

4. | Wednesday | Thursday | Friday | _____

5. | Friday | Saturday | Sunday | _____

Months of the Year

January
S M T W T F S
1 2 3
4 5 6 7 8 9 10
11 12 13 14 15 16 17
18 19 20 21 22 23 24
25 26 27 28 29 30 31

February
S M T W T F S
1 2 3 4 5 6 7
8 9 10 11 12 13 14
15 16 17 18 19 20 21
22 23 24 25 26 27 28

March
S M T W T F S
1 2 3 4 5 6 7
8 9 10 11 12 13 14
15 16 17 18 19 20 21
22 23 24 25 26 27 28
29 30 31

April
S M T W T F S
1 2 3 4
5 6 7 8 9 10 11
12 13 14 15 16 17 18
19 20 21 22 23 24 25
26 27 28 29 30

May
S M T W T F S
1 2
3 4 5 6 7 8 9
10 11 12 13 14 15 16
17 18 19 20 21 22 23
24/31 25 26 27 28 29 30

June
S M T W T F S
1 2 3 4 5 6
7 8 9 10 11 12 13
14 15 16 17 18 19 20
21 22 23 24 25 26 27
28 29 30

July
S M T W T F S
1 2 3 4
5 6 7 8 9 10 11
12 13 14 15 16 17 18
19 20 21 22 23 24 25
26 27 28 29 30 31

August
S M T W T F S
1
2 3 4 5 6 7 8
9 10 11 12 13 14 15
16 17 18 19 20 21 22
23/30 24/31 25 26 27 28 29

September
S M T W T F S
1 2 3 4 5
6 7 8 9 10 11 12
13 14 15 16 17 18 19
20 21 22 23 24 25 26
27 28 29 30

October
S M T W T F S
1 2 3
4 5 6 7 8 9 10
11 12 13 14 15 16 17
18 19 20 21 22 23 24
25 26 27 28 29 30 31

November
S M T W T F S
1 2 3 4 5 6 7
8 9 10 11 12 13 14
15 16 17 18 19 20 21
22 23 24 25 26 27 28
29 30

December
S M T W T F S
1 2 3 4 5
6 7 8 9 10 11 12
13 14 15 16 17 18 19
20 21 22 23 24 25 26
27 28 29 30 31

I. Write the names of the missing months.

January, February, _March_, _____,

_____, June, July, _____,

_____, October, _____, December

Problem Solving Number Sense

You can show the date two ways.

April 19, 2004 or **4/19/04**

The 4 tells that April is the 4th month.

2. Draw lines to match the dates.

August 22, 2004   5/9/04

May 9, 2004   8/22/04

What's Inside the Egg?

1. The zoo keeps baby tortoises in this tank. What shape is the tank?

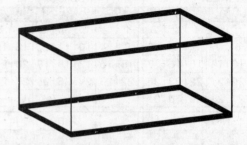

_____

2. Joan went to the zoo to see the baby tortoises. She left the zoo at 4:30. Show the time on both clocks.

3. Joan wanted to go to the zoo on Monday. Her mother took Joan the next day. On which day did Joan go to the zoo?   _____

Writing in Math

4. Joan visited the zoo in April. After 3 months, she will go back to see how much the baby tortoises have grown. Use a calendar to find which month she will return to the zoo. _____

Name _____

Numbers to 19

Use Counters and Workmat 3.

Write each number as 10 and some left over.

1. | twelve | 12 is __10__ and __2__.

2. | eighteen | 18 is _____ and _____.

3. | fourteen | 14 is _____ and _____.

4. | eleven | 11 is _____ and _____.

5. | seventeen | 17 is _____ and _____.

6. | nineteen | 19 is _____ and _____.

7. | sixteen | 16 is _____ and _____.

Problem Solving *Algebra*

Write each missing number.

8. [ ] and 10 is 13.

9. 2 and [ ] is 12.

10. 10 and [ ] is 16.

11. [ ] and 8 is 18.

12. [ ] and 10 is 17.

13. 5 and [ ] is 15.

Counting by 10s to 100

10,	20,	30,	40,	50,
ten,	twenty,	thirty,	forty,	fifty,
60,	70,	80,	90,	100
sixty,	seventy,	eighty,	ninety,	one hundred

Count by tens. Then write the numbers.

1. 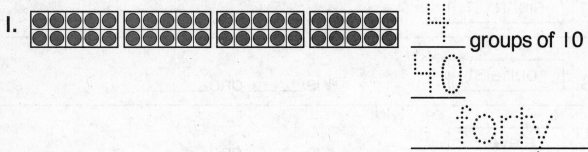 __4__ groups of 10

   40

   forty

2. 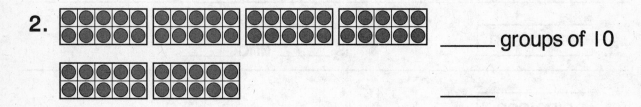 _____ groups of 10

   ____

   _____

3. 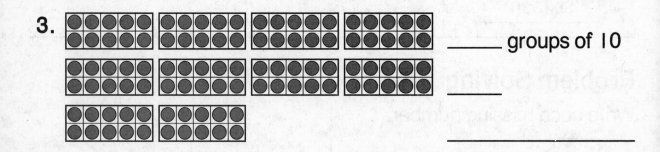 _____ groups of 10

   _____

Problem Solving *Mental Math*

4. Laura saves 10¢ each day. How much money has she saved after 5 days?

   _____ ¢

5. Kit saves 10¢ each day. How much money has he saved after 7 days?

   _____ ¢

Hundred Chart

I. Write the missing numbers. Look for patterns.

1	2								
11	12	13	14	15	16	17	18	19	20
31	32	33	34	35	36	37	38	39	40
							48	49	50
					56	57	58	59	60
61	62	63	64	65					
					76	77	78	79	80
81	82	83	84						90
91					96	97	98	99	100

Use the hundred chart above to count back by ones.

2. 79, *78*, *77*, _____, _____, _____, _____

3. 31, _____, _____, _____, _____, _____, _____

Problem Solving *Number Sense*

Look at these parts of the hundred chart.
Write the missing numbers.

4.

42			
	53		55

5.

		16	
	25		28

Counting with Groups of 10 and Leftovers

Circle groups of 10 beads.
Then write the numbers.

1.
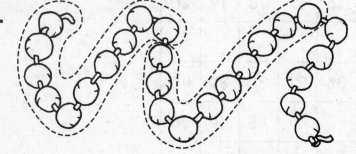

__2__ groups of 10

__5__ left over

__25__ in all

2.
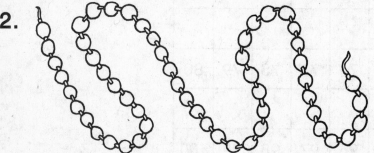

_____ groups of 10

_____ left over

_____ in all

3.
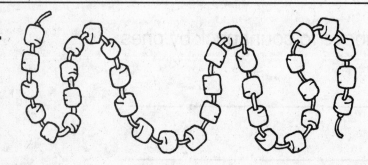

_____ groups of 10

_____ left over

_____ in all

Problem Solving *Visual Thinking*

Draw a picture to solve.

4. Ben has 25 beads. 10 beads fit on a key chain.
   How many
   key chains can he make? _____

   How many beads
   will be left over? _____

Estimating with Groups of 10

Circle a group of 10.
Then circle the best estimate for about
how many there are in all.

1.

about

20   (50)   70

2.

about

20   40   60

3.

about

10   30   50

Problem Solving *Estimation*

4. Circle all of the numbers that answer the question.

Tammy estimates that she has about 30 stamps.
Which numbers could show how many stamps
Tammy really has?

21   28   32   39   41   48   52

PROBLEM-SOLVING SKILL

Use Data from a Graph

Our Pets		
Dogs	Cats	Fish

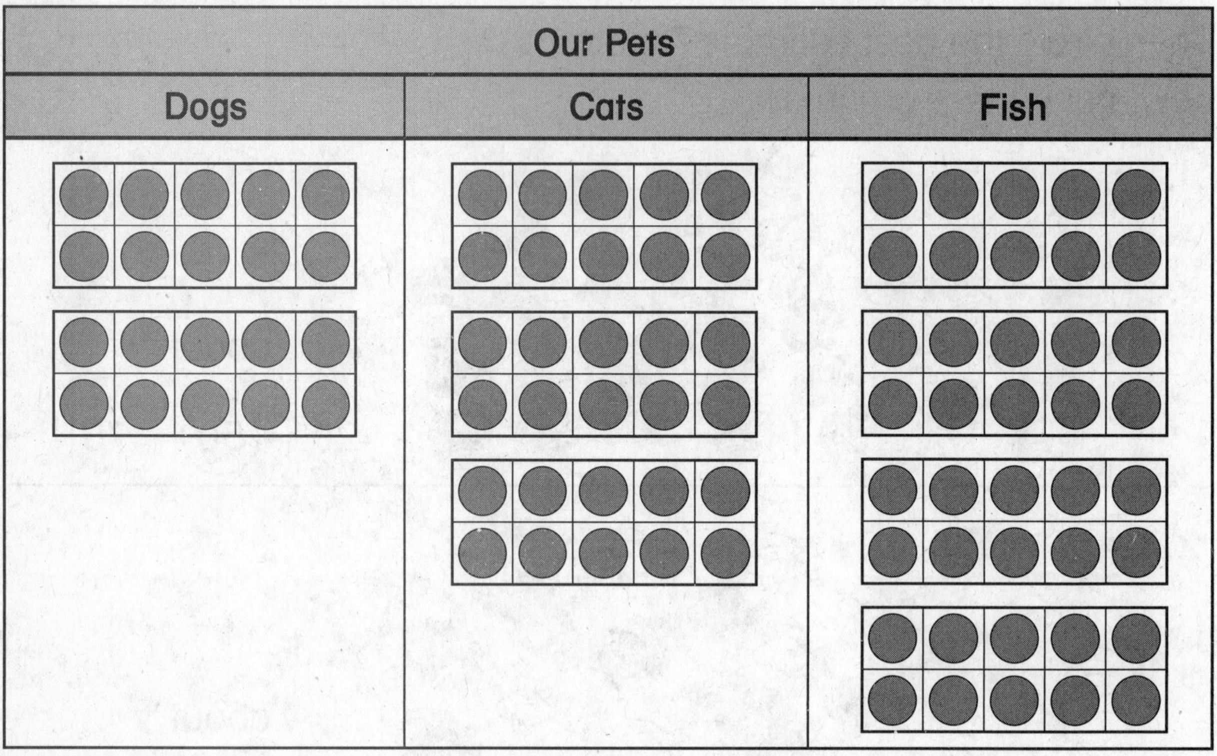

Use the graph to answer each question.

1. Of which pet are there the most? _____

2. Of which pet are there the fewest? _____

3. How many more fish are there than cats? _____

4. How many dogs and cats are there altogether? _____

Writing in Math

5. Write your own question about the graph.

_____

_____

Skip-Counting Patterns
on the Hundred Chart

1. Color the numbers you say when you count by fives.

I	2	3	4	5	6	7	8	9	10
11	12	13	14	15	16	17	18	19	20
21	22	23	24	25	26	27	28	29	30
31	32	33	34	35	36	37	38	39	40
41	42	43	44	45	46	47	48	49	50
51	52	53	54	55	56	57	58	59	60
61	62	63	64	65	66	67	68	69	70
71	72	73	74	75	76	77	78	79	80
81	82	83	84	85	86	87	88	89	90
91	92	93	94	95	96	97	98	99	100

2. Color the numbers you say when you count by twos.

61	62	63	64	65	66	67	68	69	70
71	72	73	74	75	76	77	78	79	80
81	82	83	84	85	86	87	88	89	90
91	92	93	94	95	96	97	98	99	100

Problem Solving *Visual Thinking*

Finish coloring the calendar. Write **yes** or **no.**

3. Vicki has baseball practice every 5 days.
   Will she have practice on May 19? _____

May						
Sunday	Monday	Tuesday	Wednesday	Thursday	Friday	Saturday
	I	2	3	4	5	6
7	8	9	10	11	12	13
14	15	16	17	18	19	20

Using Skip Counting

I. How many ears are there?
Count by twos.

2̲ , _____ , _____ , _____ , _____ , _____ , _____

2. How many cans are there?
Count by fives.

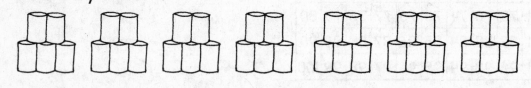

_____ , _____ , _____ , _____ , _____ , _____ , _____

3. How many balls are there?
Count by tens.

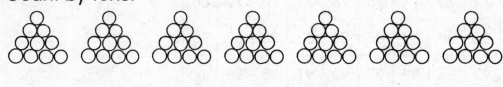

_____ , _____ , _____ , _____ , _____ , _____ , _____

Problem Solving *Algebra*

Find the pattern. Write the missing numbers.

4. 15, _____ , 25, 30, _____ , _____ , 45, _____ , _____ , 60

5. 8, _____ , 12, 14, _____ , _____ , 20, _____ , _____ , 26

6. 90, 80, 70, _____ , 50, 40, _____ , _____ , 10, 0

Name _____

Look for a Pattern

Find a pattern. Then write the numbers.

1. There are 6 butterflies. Each butterfly has 4 wings.
   How many wings are on the butterflies altogether?

Number of Butterflies	1					
Number of Wings	4					

There are _____ wings in all on the butterflies.

---

2. There are 5 cows. Each cow has 4 legs.
   How many legs are on the cows altogether?

Number of Cows					
Number of Legs					

There are _____ legs in all on the cows.

---

3. There are 7 boxes.
   Each box has 10 balls in it.
   How many balls are there altogether?

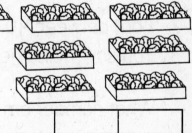

Number of Boxes						
Number of Balls						

The boxes have _____ balls in all.

Before, After, and Between

Use Workmat 6 if you like.

Write the number that is just after.

1. 41, _42_   30, _____   59, _____

2. 85, _____   28, _____   63, _____

Write the number that is just before.

3. _____, 27   _____, 51   _____, 62

4. _____, 76   _____, 45   _____, 34

Write the numbers that are in between.

5. 21, _____, _____, 24   59, _____, _____, 62

6. 45, _____, _____, 48   73, _____, _____, 76

Problem Solving *Reasoning*

Write the number that answers the riddle.

7. I am between 40 and 50.

   You say my name when you count by fives.

   What number am I? _____

8. I am between 70 and 80.

   You say my name when you count by fives.

   What number am I? _____

Odd and Even Numbers

Draw counters to show each number.
Try to make equal rows. Then circle **odd** or **even**.

1.
8

odd

(even)

2.
7

odd

even

3.
15

odd

even

4.
16

odd

even

Problem Solving *Visual Thinking*

5. Find the pattern.

Write **odd** or **even** to complete each sentence.

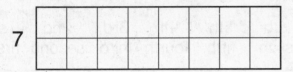

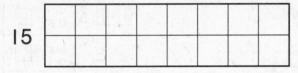

The shaded numbers are _____.

The white numbers are _____.

Ordinal Numbers Through Twentieth

1. Circle the child who is sixth in line.

Cross out the child who is ninth in line.

Draw a square around the child who is second in line.

| 10th | 9th | 8th | 7th | 6th | 5th | 4th | 3rd | 2nd | 1st |
| tenth | ninth | eighth | seventh | sixth | fifth | fourth | third | second | first |

Circle the word that completes each sentence.

2. Banji lives on the _____ floor.

second   third   fourth

3. Calvin lives on the _____ floor.

sixth   seventh   eighth

4. Samir lives on the _____ floor.

third   fourth   fifth

5. Nan lives on the _____ floor.

eighth   ninth   tenth

Andre
Nan
Erek
Li
Calvin
Samir
Agatha
Banji
Lyn
first
1st
Tom

Problem Solving *Reasoning*

6.

first second third fourth   ?   seventh eighth

How many medals are missing? _____

By the Sea

i st

1. Circle the 2nd sailboat.

2. Draw a box around the 7th sailboat.

3. Is there an even or an odd number of sailboats?

   even   odd

4. 5 people work on each sailboat. If there are
   8 sailboats in all, skip count to find how many
   people there are.

   _____ , _____ , _____ , _____ , _____ , _____ , _____ , _____

5. There are 6 sailboats.
   Each sailboat has 4 sails.
   How many sails are there in all?

Number of Sailboats					
Number of Sails					

Writing in Math

6. The family went sailing at 3:00.
   They sailed for 3 hours.
   Draw hands to show what time
   the family returned from sailing.

Numbers Made with Tens

Count the tens. Then write the numbers.

1. _____ tens is _____.

2. _____ tens is _____.

3. _____ tens is _____.

4. _____ tens is _____.

5. _____ tens is _____.

6. _____ tens is _____.

Problem Solving *Mental Math*

7. Nancy has 50 marbles.
   30 of the marbles are in one bag.
   The rest are in the second bag.
   How many marbles are in the
   second bag?

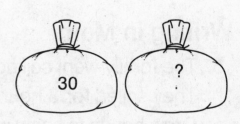

_____

Name _____

Tens and Ones

Count the tens and ones. Then write the numbers.

1.

Tens	Ones

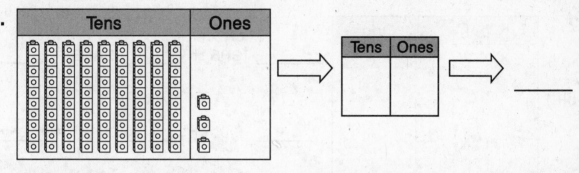

Tens	Ones
4	5

45

2.

Tens	Ones

Tens	Ones

_____

3.

Tens	Ones

Tens	Ones

_____

Problem Solving *Visual Thinking*

4. Javier wants to show 66 with models. Draw the
missing models to help Javier show 66.

Expanded Form

Draw the tens and ones. Then write the numbers.

1.

Tens	Ones

(36)

___3___ tens + ___6___ ones = __36__

__30__ + ___6___ = __36__

2.

Tens	Ones

(54)

_____ tens + _____ ones = _____

_____ + _____ = _____

3.

Tens	Ones

(69)

_____ tens + _____ ones = _____

_____ + _____ = _____

Problem Solving *Reasoning*

Write the number that matches the clues.

4. The digit in the tens place is **even**,
and it is greater than 6.
The digit in the ones place is **odd**,
and it is between 3 and 7.

Tens	Ones

Ways to Make Numbers

Use cubes and Workmat 4 to show a different
way to make the number.

1.

Tens	Ones

$37 = 30 + 7$

Break apart a ten into 10 ones.

$37 = \underline{20} + \underline{17}$

2.

Tens	Ones

$24 = 10 + 14$

Make a ten with 10 ones.

$24 = \underline{} + \underline{}$

3.

Tens	Ones

$62 = 60 + 2$

Break apart a ten into 10 ones.

$62 = \underline{} + \underline{}$

Problem Solving *Number Sense*

Use cubes to solve. Circle **yes** or **no**.

4. On Mario's workmat there are
4 tens and 8 ones. On Jeb's
workmat there are 3 tens and
18 ones. Are the boys showing
the same number on their workmats?

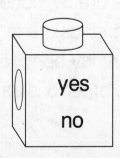

yes

no

PROBLEM SOLVING STRATEGY

Use Objects

Use cubes to find how many there are in all.

1. How many potatoes are there in all?

   ⠒⠃⠒ potatoes   23 potatoes   13 potatoes

2. How many apples are there in all?

   _____ apples   24 apples   25 apples

3. How many tomatoes are there in all?

   _____ tomatoes   57 tomatoes   11 tomatoes

4. How many oranges are there in all?

   _____ oranges   35 oranges   22 oranges

Problem Solving *Algebra*

Use cubes. Write the number
of bananas below the basket.

5. There are 37 bananas in all.
   21 bananas are in one basket.
   How many bananas are there
   in the other basket?

   21 bananas   _____ bananas

1 More, 1 Less;
10 More, 10 Less

Use cubes. Write the numbers.

1.

1 more than 35 is _36_ .

10 less than 35 is _25_ .

2.

10 more than 26 is _____ .

1 less than 26 is _____ .

3.

10 less than 42 is _____ .

1 more than 42 is _____ .

4.

1 less than 70 is _____ .

10 more than 70 is _____ .

Problem Solving *Reasoning*

5. Stan, Don, and Tom got their team shirts.

Use the clues to write the number of each boy's shirt.

The number on Stan's shirt is 10 less than Don's.

The number on Don's shirt is 1 more than Tom's.

Tom's number is 16.

_____   _____   _____
Stan   Don   Tom

Comparing Numbers: Greater Than, Less Than, Equal

Write <, >, or =.

1.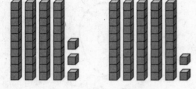

43 is ⸰less than⸰ 52.

43 Ⓒ 52

2.

65 is _____ 37.

65 ◯ 37

< less than	> greater than	= equal to

Write <, >, or =.

3. 27 Ⓔ 27

4. 45 ◯ 50

5. 59 ◯ 41

6. 35 ◯ 53

Problem Solving *Visual Thinking*

7. Draw different models in the empty box.
Make both sides equal.

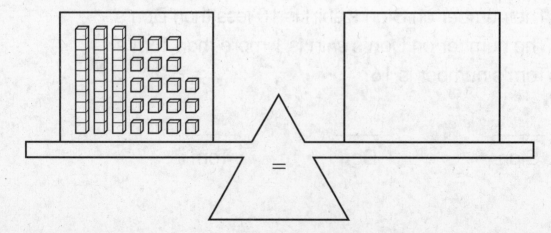

Number-Line Estimation: Numbers to 100

Complete the number line.
Then draw lines to show where the numbers go.

1.

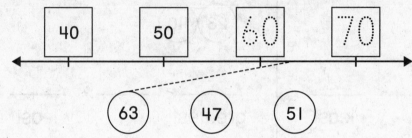

2.

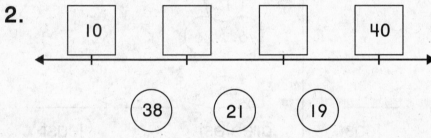

3.

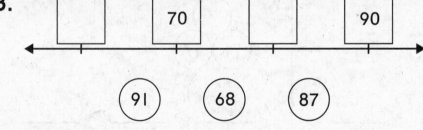

Problem Solving *Estimation*

4. Draw lines to show where the numbers go.

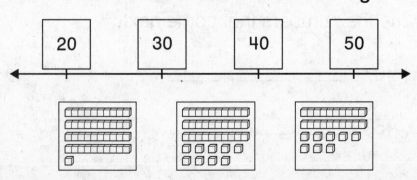

Name _____

Ordering Three Numbers

Write the numbers in order from **greatest** to **least**.
Use a hundred chart if you like.

1.
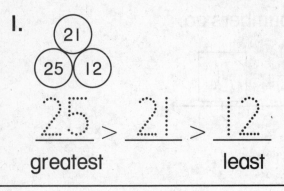

25 > 21 > 12
greatest   least

2.
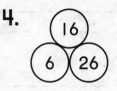

____ > ____ > ____
greatest   least

3.

(60)
(56) (65)

____ > ____ > ____
greatest   least

4.

(16)
(6) (26)

____ > ____ > ____
greatest   least

5.

(62)
(36) (46)

____ > ____ > ____
greatest   least

6.

(7)
(71) (17)

____ > ____ > ____
greatest   least

Problem Solving *Algebra*

Find the pattern. Write the numbers that come next.

7. 20, 25, 30, 35, 40, _____, _____, _____

8. 65, 60, 55, 50, 45, _____, _____, _____

Hundreds

Write how many hundreds, tens, and ones there are.
Then write the number.

I.

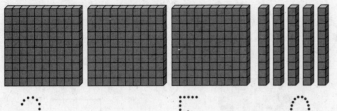

__3__ hundreds __5__ tens __0__ ones = __350__

2.

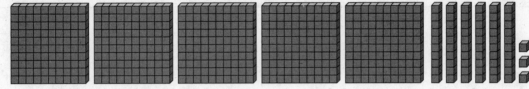

_____ hundreds _____ tens _____ ones = _____

3.

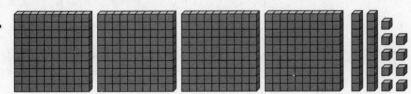

_____ hundreds _____ tens _____ ones = _____

Problem Solving *Visual Thinking*

4. Write the missing numbers in the chart.

491				495		497		499	
	502	503				507			510
511			514					519	
521		523		525				529	530

Sorting

How could you sort these shapes?
Draw and color to show two groups you could make.

1.

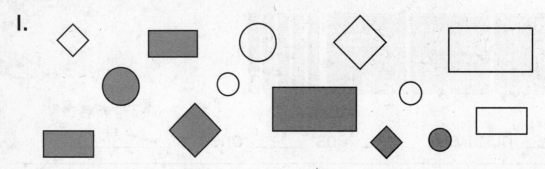

Problem Solving *Reasoning*

Circle the shape that does not belong in the group.

2.

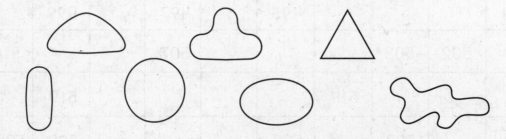

Name _____

Making Graphs

1. Ask your class to select their favorite snack.
   Draw to make a picture graph.
   Then answer the questions.

Our Favorite Snacks		
△	⬭	🍿
Pizza	Peanuts	Popcorn

2. Which snack is the
   favorite of the class?

   _____

3. Which snack is the
   least favorite?

   _____

4. How many children would
   have selected pizza if
   2 more children had selected it?

   _____

Problem Solving *Writing in Math*

5. Write a question about the picture graph above.

   _____

   _____

Name _____

Making Bar Graphs

1. Ask your classmates to select their favorite sticker.
   Color to make a bar graph.
   Then answer the questions.

2. Which sticker is the favorite
   of the class?

   _____

3. Which sticker is the
   least favorite?

   _____

4. How many children would
   have selected the bird sticker
   if 1 more child had selected it?

   _____

Our Favorite Stickers

	10			
9			
8			
7			
6			
5			
4			
3			
2			
1			
	Flowers	Birds	Dinosaurs

Problem Solving *Number Sense*

5. Put the stickers in order from **least** to **greatest**
   according to the number of spaces colored.
   Write the words **Flowers, Birds,** and **Dinosaurs.**

   _____ , _____ , _____

   least   **greatest**

Using Tally Marks

Write tally marks to show how many flowers
there are of each kind. Write the totals.

			Total
Rose			
Tulip			
Daisy			

Use the tally chart to answer the questions.

I. Of which flower are there the fewest? _____

2. How many daisies and roses are there altogether? _____

3. How many more daisies than tulips are there? _____

Problem Solving *Writing in Math*

4. Write your own question about the tally chart above.

_____

_____

Coordinate Grids

This is a map of Malik's town.

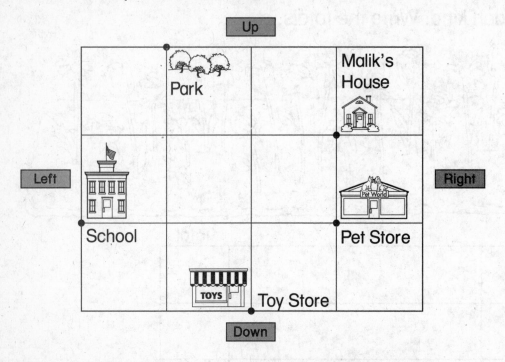

Read the map. Then complete each sentence.

1. To go from the 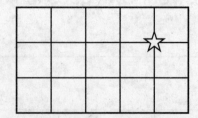 to the ,

go __2__ blocks right and __2__ blocks down.

---

2. To go from the to the ,

go _____ blocks left and _____ block up.

Problem Solving *Visual Thinking*

3. Start at the ☆.
Move 4 spaces to the left
and 1 space down.
Draw a circle.

Use Data from a Map

Green Park

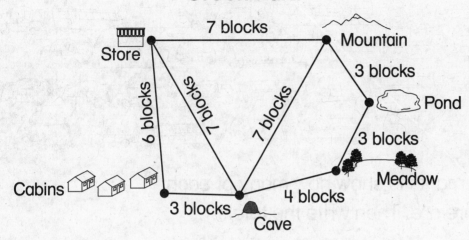

How many blocks is it? Find the shortest path.
Then write an addition sentence.

1. From the 🏠🏠🏠 to the ⛰

   __3__ + __7__ = __10__ blocks

2. From the ☁ to the 🏪

   _____ + _____ = _____ blocks

3. From the 🏠🏠🏠 to the 🌳🌳

   _____ + _____ = _____ blocks

4. From the ⛰ to the ☁

   _____ + _____ = _____ blocks

5. From the ⛰ to the 🌳🌳

   _____ + _____ = _____ blocks

PROBLEM-SOLVING APPLICATIONS

Let's Make Soup!

1. Make tally marks to show how many of each
vehicle there are. Then write the totals.

Car		
Bus		
Truck		

2. Write the numbers of vehicles in order
from **least** to **greatest**.

____ < ____ < ____

least   greatest

Writing in Math

3. Make a picture graph
that shows how many
of each vehicle
are on this page.

Nickel and Penny

Count on. Then write how much money in all.

1.

5 ¢   6 ¢   7 ¢   8 ¢   9 ¢

In All
9 ____ ¢

2.

____ ¢ ____ ¢ ____ ¢ ____ ¢ ____ ¢

In All
____ ¢

Circle the coins that match each price.

3. 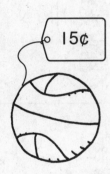 15¢

4.  13¢

Problem Solving *Algebra*

5. Write the price for each toy.
   Remember, the price of the
   sailboat must stay the same.

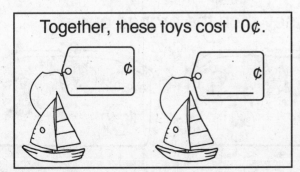

Together, these toys cost 10¢.

Together, these toys cost 8¢.

Name _____

Dime

P 9-2

Count on. Then write how much money in all.

1.

10¢ 20¢ 30¢ 31¢ 32¢

In All
32¢

2.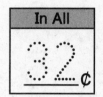

___¢ ___¢ ___¢ ___¢ ___¢ ___¢ ___¢

In All
___¢

Circle the coins that match each price.

3.  61¢

4. 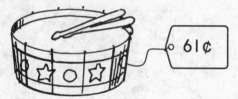 33¢

Problem Solving *Number Sense*

5. Color each change purse to match the clues.

The yellow purse has the most money.

The blue purse has more money than the orange purse.

106 Use with Lesson 9-2.

Counting Dimes and Nickels

Count on. Then write how much money in all.

1.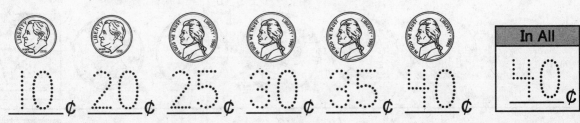

.10. ¢ .20. ¢ .25. ¢ .30. ¢ .35. ¢ .40. ¢   In All 40 ¢

2.

____¢ ____¢ ____¢ ____¢ ____¢ ____¢ ____¢   In All ____¢

Write how much money in all.
Then circle the toy that you can buy.

3.    In All 60 ¢   65¢ 60¢

4.   In All ____¢   70¢ 75¢

Problem Solving *Number Sense*

Solve the riddles.

5. Hayes has 5 coins. She has 2 dimes. The rest are nickels. How much money does Hayes have?

____¢

6. Jake has 5 coins. He has 2 nickels. The rest are dimes. How much money does Jake have?

____¢

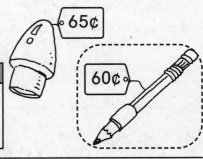

Counting Dimes, Nickels, and Pennies

Count on. Then write how much money in all.

1.

In All
37¢

2.

In All
____ ¢

3.

In All
____ ¢

4.

In All
____ ¢

Problem Solving *Algebra*

5. There are five coins in Dan's bank.
   Some are dimes, and some are nickels.
   What is the greatest amount
   of money Dan could have? _____ ¢
   What is the least amount
   of money Dan could have? _____ ¢

Use Data from a Table

Use the menu. Write **yes** or **no**.

Menu

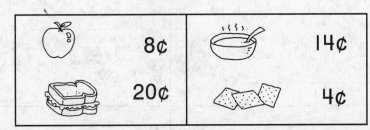

You Buy	You Use	Will you get change?
1.		
2.		
3.		

Problem Solving *Writing in Math*

4. Write a story problem using information
   from the menu.

_____

_____

_____

Quarter

Circle the coins that equal 25¢.

1.

2.

3.

4.

5.

Problem Solving *Visual Thinking*

6. Lucia has 4 coins in her purse.

They are worth 25¢ in all.

Draw and label Lucia's coins.

Counting Sets of Coins

Count on. Then write how much money in all.

1.

25 ¢ 35 ¢ 40 ¢ 45 ¢ 50 ¢ 51 ¢ 52 ¢ | In All |
| 52 ¢ |

2.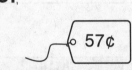

___ ¢ ___ ¢ ___ ¢ ___ ¢ ___ ¢ ___ ¢ | In All |
| ___ ¢ |

Circle the coins that match each amount.

3. 57¢

4. 53¢

Problem Solving *Reasoning*

5. How can you show the same amount using fewer coins?
Draw and label the coins in the empty change purse.

 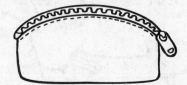

Half-Dollar and Dollar

Write how much money in all.

1.

In All
$1.00

2.

In All
_____

3.

In All
_____

Problem Solving *Reasoning*

4. How can you show the same amount using only
   2 coins? Draw and label the coins in the empty bank.

Try, Check, and Revise

Circle the stickers each child bought.
Then write an addition sentence to check your guess.

4¢   5¢   9¢   8¢

---

1. Venus bought 2 different stickers.
Together they cost 14¢.
What did Venus buy?

 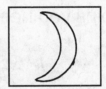

_____ + _____ = _____¢

---

2. Carlos bought 2 different stickers.
Together they cost 9¢.
What did Carlos buy?

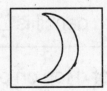 

_____ + _____ = _____¢

---

3. Anita bought 2 different stickers.
Together they cost 12¢.
What did Anita buy?

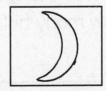 

_____ + _____ = _____¢

Name _____

PROBLEM-SOLVING APPLICATIONS P 9-10

What Can You Buy?

1. Circle the coins you need to buy 1 top.

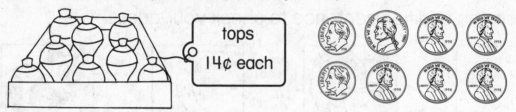

tops
14¢ each

2. Circle the coins you need to buy 1 pencil.

pencils
9¢ each

3. Circle the coins you need to buy 2 pencils.

Write **less than** or **greater than**.

4. The price of a pencil is _____ the price of a top.

5. Is the price of a top an odd number
   or an even number? _____

Problem Solving *Writing in Math*

6. Each balloon costs 5 cents. You have a quarter to spend on balloons. How many balloons can you buy? Explain.

_____

114 Use with Lesson 9-10.

Estimating, Measuring, and Comparing Length

Find each object in your classroom.
Estimate the length. Then measure using cubes.

1. ERASER	Estimate.	Measure.
	about _____	about _____
2. (crayon)	about _____	about _____
3. (paper clip)	about _____	about _____

Problem Solving *Visual Thinking*

4. Measure each bug using cubes. Circle the longest bug.
   Mark an **X** on the shortest bug.

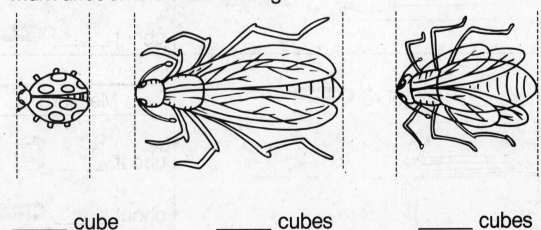

_____ cube   _____ cubes   _____ cubes

Use Logical Reasoning

Will it take fewer snap cubes or fewer paper clips
to measure the objects below?
Circle your prediction. Then measure.

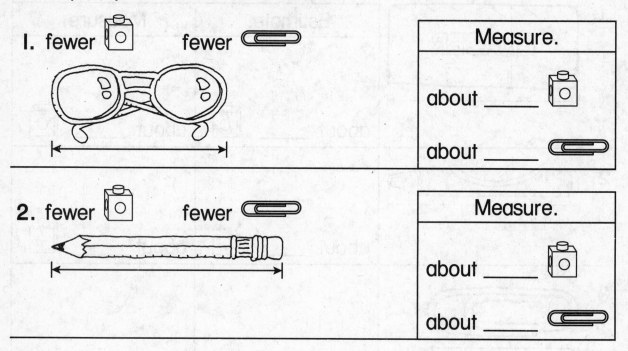

1. fewer 🔲   fewer ⬭

Measure.
about _____ 🔲
about _____ ⬭

2. fewer 🔲   fewer ⬭

Measure.
about _____ 🔲
about _____ ⬭

Will it take more snap cubes or more paper clips to measure
the objects below? Circle your prediction. Then measure.

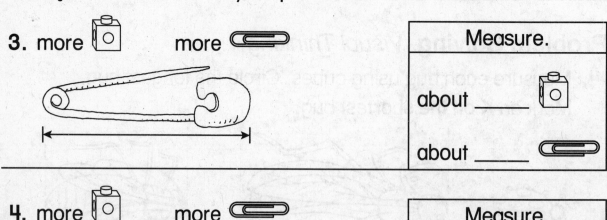

3. more 🔲   more ⬭

Measure.
about _____ 🔲
about _____ ⬭

4. more 🔲   more ⬭

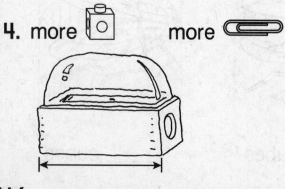

Measure.
about _____ 🔲
about _____ ⬭

Estimating and Measuring with Inches P 10-3

Find each object in your classroom.
Estimate the length or height.
Then measure using a ruler.

	Estimate.	Measure.
1.	about ____ inches	about ____ inches
2.	about ____ inches	about ____ inches
3.	about ____ inches	about ____ inches

Problem Solving *Mental Math*

Answer the questions.

4. This stamp is 1 inch long.

How long are 4 stamps? ____ inches

How long are 6 stamps? ____ inches

Estimating and Measuring with Feet

Find each object in your classroom.
Estimate the length or height.
Then measure using a ruler.

	Estimate.	Measure.
1.	about _____ feet	about _____ feet
2.	about _____ feet	about _____ feet
3.	about _____ feet	about _____ feet

Problem Solving *Reasonableness*

4. About how long might each object be?
Circle the better estimate.

about 3 inches   about 3 feet

about 2 inches   about 2 feet

5. Draw a box around the shorter object.

Estimating and Measuring with Centimeters

Find each object in your classroom.
Estimate the length. Then measure
using a centimeter ruler.

1.

	Estimate.	Measure.
	about _____ centimeters	about _____ centimeters
2.	about _____ centimeters	about _____ centimeters
3.	about _____ centimeters	about _____ centimeters

Problem Solving *Reasonableness*

Are these objects taller or shorter than 10 centimeters?
Circle the better choice.

4.

taller than 10 centimeters

shorter than 10 centimeters

5.

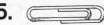

taller than 10 centimeters

shorter than 10 centimeters

Understanding Perimeter

Count how many inches around each shape.

1.

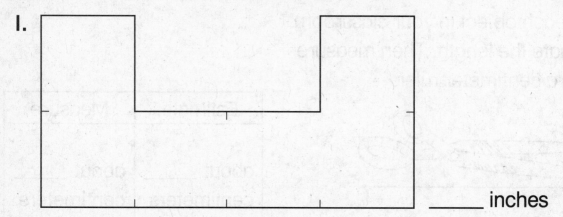

_____ inches

2.

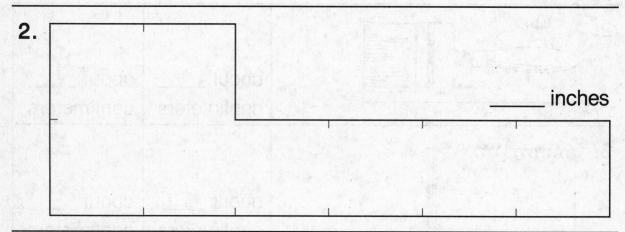

_____ inches

Problem Solving *Mental Math*

3. Maggie measured 6 inches around this shape.
How many inches long is each side?

2 inches

_____ inch   _____ inch

_____ inches

PROBLEM-SOLVING SKILL

Look Back and Check

How many cubes will cover each shape?
Circle the answer that makes sense.

1.

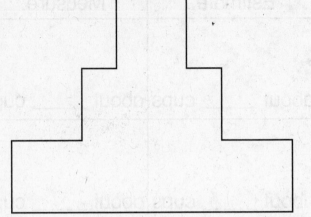

7 cubes

12 cubes

2.

8 cubes

10 cubes

Problem Solving *Visual Thinking*

3. Draw a different shape with the same number
of square units.

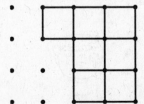

Estimating, Measuring, and Comparing Capacity

Estimate how many cups of rice will fill each item.
Then measure.

	Estimate.	Measure.
1.	about _____ cups	about _____ cups
2.	about _____ cups	about _____ cups
3.	about _____ cups	about _____ cups
4.	about _____ cups	about _____ cups

Problem Solving *Estimation*

5. Circle the container that holds about 2 cups.

Cups, Pints, and Quarts

Circle the best estimate.

1.  (more than I pint)

less than I pint

2.  more than I cup

less than I cup

3.  more than I cup

less than I cup

4.   more than I quart

less than I quart

5.  more than I pint

less than I pint

6.  more than I cup

less than I cup

Problem Solving *Reasoning*

Fill in each blank.

7. I pint = 2 cups

2 pints = _____ cups

8. I quart = 2 pints

2 quarts = _____ pints

Name _____

Liters

Circle the best estimate.

1.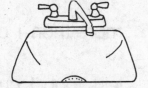

less than I liter

(more than I liter)

2.

less than I liter

more than I liter

3.

less than I liter

more than I liter

4.

less than I liter

more than I liter

5.

less than I liter

more than I liter

6.

less than I liter

more than I liter

Problem Solving *Estimation*

Circle the best estimate.

7.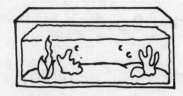

I liter

10 liters

8.

I liter

10 liters

124 Use with Lesson 10-10.

Estimating, Measuring, and Comparing Weight

Estimate how many cubes it will take to balance.
Then measure.

	Estimate.	Measure.
1.	about _____ 🧊	about _____ 🧊
2.	about _____ 🧊	about _____ 🧊
3.	about _____ 🧊	about _____ 🧊

Problem Solving *Number Sense*

4. Number the objects from lightest to heaviest.
Use **1** for the lightest and **4** for the heaviest.

_____ _____ _____ _____

Name _____

Pounds

Circle the best estimate.

1. less than 1 pound

(more than 1 pound)

2. less than 1 pound

more than 1 pound

3. less than 1 pound

more than 1 pound

4. less than 1 pound

more than 1 pound

5. less than 1 pound

more than 1 pound

6. less than 1 pound

more than 1 pound

7. less than 1 pound

more than 1 pound

8. less than 1 pound

more than 1 pound

Problem Solving *Mental Math*

Count by 10s to solve.

9. The class buys 8 pounds of apples.
Each pound costs 10¢.

How much does the class pay? _____ ¢

Name _____

Grams and Kilograms

Circle the best estimate.

1.

(grams)

kilograms

2.

grams

kilograms

3.

grams

kilograms

4.

grams

kilograms

5.

grams

kilograms

6.

grams

kilograms

7.

grams

kilograms

8.

grams

kilograms

Problem Solving *Algebra*

Solve.

9. Cindy has two puppies.
Together they measure 7 kilograms.
One puppy measures 3 kilograms.
How much does the other puppy measure?

$3 +$ _____ $= 7$ kilograms

Name _____

Measuring Temperature

Circle the thermometer that shows the temperature.

1.

28°F   80°F

2.

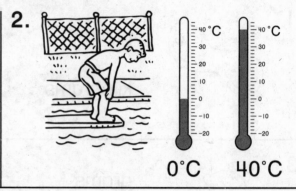

0°C   40°C

Draw lines to match each picture to the temperature.

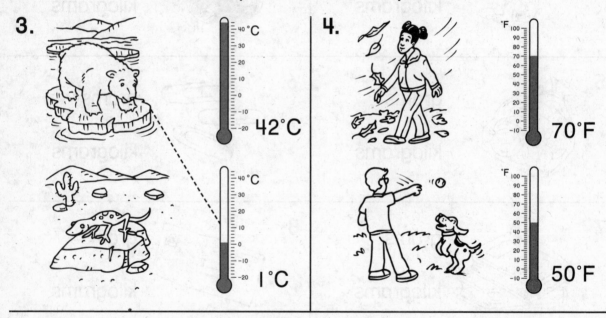

3.

42°C

1°C

4.

70°F

50°F

Problem Solving *Number Sense*

5. Number the thermometers from coldest to hottest.
   Use **1** for coldest and **3** for hottest.

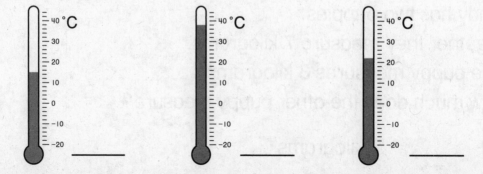

_____   _____   _____

Choosing a Measurement Tool

Circle the best tool to use for the measurement.

1. How hot is it?

2. How long is it?

3. How much will it hold?

4. How heavy is it?

 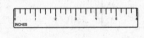

Problem Solving *Reasoning*

Draw something you could measure with each tool.

5.

6.

Certain or Impossible

Color the cubes so that each sentence is true.

1. You are certain to pick a blue cube.

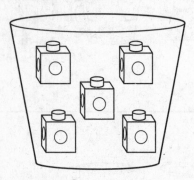

2. It is impossible to pick a red cube.

3. It is impossible to pick a green cube.

4. You are certain to pick a yellow cube.

Problem Solving *Visual Thinking*

5. Draw 5 cubes in the bag. Color the cubes so that it is impossible to pick a blue cube **and** you are certain to pick a red cube.

Name _____

More Likely or Less Likely

Use each tally chart to answer the questions.

1.

Color	Tally
Black	IIII
White	IIII III

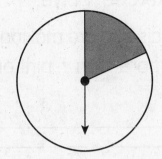

Predict:

On which color is the spinner
more likely to land on next? _____

2.

Color	Tally
Black	IIII I
White	IIII IIII II

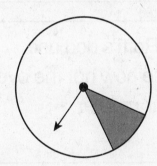

Predict:

On which color is the spinner
less likely to land on next? _____

Problem Solving *Algebra*

Solve.

3. Tony spun this spinner 12 times.
He landed on white 3 times.
How many times did he
land on black?

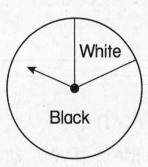

_____

Name _____

Stir-Fry It!

Read each exercise. Solve.

1. Raffi and his dad are making bread. Raffi measures 1 cup of milk.
   Is 1 cup more than 1 pint or less than 1 pint?

   _____

2. The bread pan measures 8 inches. Is the bread pan
   more than 1 foot long or less than 1 foot long?

   _____

3. What will Raffi's dad use
   to measure how hot the oven is?
   Circle your answer.

   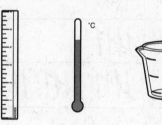

   _____

4. It takes a half hour to make chow mein. It takes 2 hours
   to make bread. Which takes longer to make?

   _____

5. Raffi wants to have milk to drink with his bread.
   Will he have more than 1 liter or less than 1 liter?

   _____

Writing in Math

6. Ask 10 children in your class if they prefer bagels or muffins.
   Make a tally chart to show their answers.

Doubles

Circle the doubles. Then add.

1. 5   6   6   8   5   2
   +5   +7   +3   +8   +8   +2
   ____   ____   ____   ____   ____   ____

2. 4   2   7   8   4   5
   +2   +7   +7   +1   +4   +2
   ____   ____   ____   ____   ____   ____

3. 7   5   3   6   9   4
   +1   +0   +3   +9   +2   +4
   ____   ____   ____   ____   ____   ____

4. 6   5   6   9   5   1
   +6   +7   +8   +9   +4   +1
   ____   ____   ____   ____   ____   ____

Problem Solving *Visual Thinking*

5. For each picture write an addition sentence
   that tells how many fingers are showing in all.

____ + ____ = ____   ____ + ____ = ____

Doubles Plus I and Doubles Minus I

Add the doubles.

Then use the doubles to help you add.

1.

Think

$5 + 5 = 10$

so $5 + 6 = 11$

and $5 + 4 = 9$

2.

Think

$3 + 3 = $ _____

so $3 + 4 = $ _____

and $3 + 2 = $ _____

3.

Think

$7 + 7 = $ _____

so $7 + 8 = $ _____

and $7 + 6 = $ _____

4.

Think

$8 + 8 = $ _____

so $8 + 9 = $ _____

and $8 + 7 = $ _____

Problem Solving *Mental Math*

Answer each question.

5. Paco has 5 model cars.
He gets 6 more cars for his
birthday. How many cars
does he have now?

_____ model cars

6. Lynn picks 5 tulips.
She picks 4 daisies.
How many flowers did
she pick in all?

_____ flowers

Name _____

Adding 10

Draw the counters. Then find the sum.

1.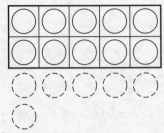

$$10 + 6 = \underline{\hspace{1cm}}$$

2.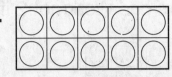

$$10 + 4 = \underline{\hspace{1cm}}$$

Write the addition problem for each ten-frame.

3.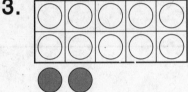

$$\begin{array}{r} 10 \\ +\ 2 \\ \hline 12 \end{array}$$

4.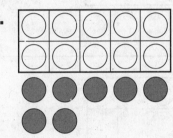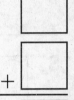

$$\begin{array}{r} \square \\ +\ \square \\ \hline \square \end{array}$$

5.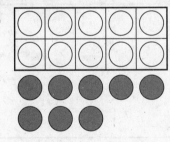

$$\begin{array}{r} \square \\ +\ \square \\ \hline \square \end{array}$$

6.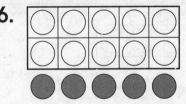

$$\begin{array}{r} \square \\ +\ \square \\ \hline \square \end{array}$$

Problem Solving *Algebra*

7. Find the pattern. Then write the missing numbers.

4	5	□	7	□	9
+ 10	+ □	+ 10	+ □	+ 10	+ □
□	15	16	17	18	□

Making 10 to Add

Draw the counters. Then write the sums.
Use counters and Workmat 2 if you like.

1.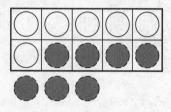

$$\begin{array}{r} 6 \\ +\ 7 \\ \hline 13 \end{array}$$

$$\begin{array}{r} 10 \\ +\ 3 \\ \hline 13 \end{array}$$

2.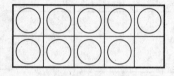

$$\begin{array}{r} 9 \\ +\ 5 \\ \hline \end{array}$$

$$\begin{array}{r} 10 \\ +\ 4 \\ \hline \end{array}$$

3.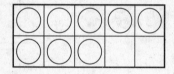

$$\begin{array}{r} 8 \\ +\ 3 \\ \hline \end{array}$$

$$\begin{array}{r} 10 \\ +\ 1 \\ \hline \end{array}$$

4.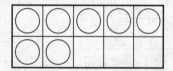

$$\begin{array}{r} 7 \\ +\ 5 \\ \hline \end{array}$$

$$\begin{array}{r} 10 \\ +\ 2 \\ \hline \end{array}$$

Problem Solving *Algebra*

Complete each number sentence.

5. $7 + 6 = 10 + 3 =$ ▢

6. $8 + 7 = 10 + 5 =$ ▢

7. $9 + 9 = 10 + 8 =$ ▢

Applying Addition Fact Strategies

Add.

1.
$$\begin{array}{r} 5 \\ + 9 \\ \hline \end{array}$$
$$\begin{array}{r} 6 \\ + 7 \\ \hline \end{array}$$
$$\begin{array}{r} 5 \\ + 6 \\ \hline \end{array}$$
$$\begin{array}{r} 6 \\ + 8 \\ \hline \end{array}$$
$$\begin{array}{r} 4 \\ + 8 \\ \hline \end{array}$$
$$\begin{array}{r} 9 \\ + 7 \\ \hline \end{array}$$

2.
$$\begin{array}{r} 9 \\ + 2 \\ \hline \end{array}$$
$$\begin{array}{r} 5 \\ + 7 \\ \hline \end{array}$$
$$\begin{array}{r} 7 \\ + 7 \\ \hline \end{array}$$
$$\begin{array}{r} 8 \\ + 7 \\ \hline \end{array}$$
$$\begin{array}{r} 9 \\ + 3 \\ \hline \end{array}$$
$$\begin{array}{r} 5 \\ + 8 \\ \hline \end{array}$$

3.
$$\begin{array}{r} 7 \\ + 6 \\ \hline \end{array}$$
$$\begin{array}{r} 8 \\ + 5 \\ \hline \end{array}$$
$$\begin{array}{r} 3 \\ + 7 \\ \hline \end{array}$$
$$\begin{array}{r} 6 \\ + 9 \\ \hline \end{array}$$
$$\begin{array}{r} 9 \\ + 4 \\ \hline \end{array}$$
$$\begin{array}{r} 4 \\ + 7 \\ \hline \end{array}$$

4.
$$\begin{array}{r} 9 \\ + 5 \\ \hline \end{array}$$
$$\begin{array}{r} 8 \\ + 9 \\ \hline \end{array}$$
$$\begin{array}{r} 6 \\ + 6 \\ \hline \end{array}$$
$$\begin{array}{r} 8 \\ + 3 \\ \hline \end{array}$$
$$\begin{array}{r} 4 \\ + 9 \\ \hline \end{array}$$
$$\begin{array}{r} 7 \\ + 5 \\ \hline \end{array}$$

Problem Solving *Writing in Math*

5. Write a story problem that can be
solved by making ten to add.
Then explain how to solve the problem.

_____

_____

Adding Three Numbers

Circle the two numbers you add first.
Then find the sum.

1.
  (8)
  3
+(2)
—
13
  [10]

  7
  4
+ 3
  [ ]

  9
  1
+ 5
  [ ]

2.
  6
  3
+ 4
  [ ]

  5
  5
+ 7
  [ ]

  2
  8
+ 7
  [ ]

Problem Solving *Algebra*

3. The three numbers on
each branch add up to 12.
Find the missing numbers.

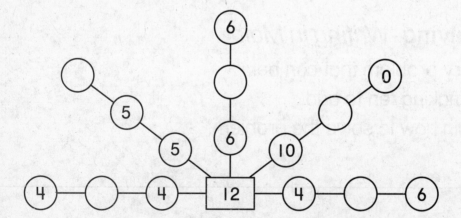

Name _____

Make a Table

Make a table to solve the problem.

1. José is making snack packs. He has bags of raisins, nuts, and pretzels. Each snack pack has 3 bags. How many different snack packs can José make?

   There are _____ different ways.

Raisins	Nuts	Pretzels
3	0	0

Reasoning

2. What do you notice about the sum of each column of the table?

_____

_____

Name _____

Using Related Facts

Write related addition and subtraction
facts for each picture.

1.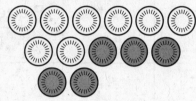

$$\underline{8} + \underline{5} = \underline{13}$$
$$\underline{13} - \underline{5} = \underline{8}$$

2.

$$\underline{} + \underline{} = \underline{}$$
$$\underline{} - \underline{} = \underline{}$$

3.

$$\underline{} + \underline{} = \underline{}$$
$$\underline{} - \underline{} = \underline{}$$

4.

$$\underline{} + \underline{} = \underline{}$$
$$\underline{} - \underline{} = \underline{}$$

Problem Solving *Number Sense*

Write two related facts to answer the questions.

5. There are 7 blue balloons and 8 red balloons.

How many balloons are there in all? $\underline{} + \underline{} = \underline{}$

If 8 balloons break,
how many balloons are left now? $\underline{} - \underline{} = \underline{}$

Fact Families

Complete each fact family.

1.

$6 + 7 =$ _____

_____ $+$ _____ $=$ _____

$13 - 7 =$ _____

_____ $-$ _____ $=$ _____

Use the numbers on each fish to write a fact family.

2.

_____ $+$ _____ $=$ _____

_____ $+$ _____ $=$ _____

_____ $-$ _____ $=$ _____

_____ $-$ _____ $=$ _____

3.

_____ $+$ _____ $=$ _____

_____ $+$ _____ $=$ _____

_____ $-$ _____ $=$ _____

_____ $-$ _____ $=$ _____

Problem Solving *Algebra*

Write the missing number for each fact family.

4. 15 _____ 9

5. $5 \ 13$ _____

Using Addition to Subtract

Circle the addition fact that will help you subtract. Then subtract.

1. $12 - 5 = \underline{7}$

$(5 + 7 = 12)$

$5 + 6 = 11$

2. $17 - 9 = \underline{\hspace{1cm}}$

$9 + 7 = 16$

$8 + 9 = 17$

3. $11 - 4 = \underline{\hspace{1cm}}$

$4 + 6 = 10$

$4 + 7 = 11$

4. $13 - 8 = \underline{\hspace{1cm}}$

$5 + 9 = 14$

$8 + 5 = 13$

5. $16 - 8 = \underline{\hspace{1cm}}$

$8 + 8 = 16$

$8 + 9 = 17$

6. $15 - 6 = \underline{\hspace{1cm}}$

$6 + 10 = 16$

$9 + 6 = 15$

Problem Solving *Mental Math*

Solve.

7. Roger does 8 of his 15 math problems.
How many problems does Roger still need to do?

_____ problems

Name _____

Using 10 to Subtract

Cross out to subtract.
Use a ten-frame and counters if you like.

1.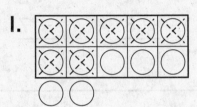
$\begin{array}{r} 12 \\ -\ 7 \\ \hline 5 \end{array}$

2.
$\begin{array}{r} 16 \\ -\ 9 \\ \hline \end{array}$

3.
$\begin{array}{r} 15 \\ -\ 6 \\ \hline \end{array}$

4.
$\begin{array}{r} 14 \\ -\ 7 \\ \hline \end{array}$

5.
$\begin{array}{r} 18 \\ -\ 9 \\ \hline \end{array}$

6.
$\begin{array}{r} 15 \\ -\ 7 \\ \hline \end{array}$

7.
$\begin{array}{r} 17 \\ -\ 9 \\ \hline \end{array}$

8.
$\begin{array}{r} 17 \\ -\ 8 \\ \hline \end{array}$

Problem Solving *Estimation*

Circle your answer.

9. You bought some juice.
You gave the clerk a dime
and a few nickels. How much
did the juice probably cost?

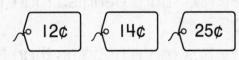
12¢   14¢   25¢

Applying Subtraction Fact Strategies **P 11-12**

Subtract.

1.	14 $-\ 9$	13 $-\ 5$	15 $-\ 7$	16 $-\ 8$	11 $-\ 8$	12 $-\ 7$

2.	18 $-\ 9$	15 $-\ 6$	14 $-\ 5$	16 $-\ 9$	11 $-\ 3$	15 $-\ 8$

3.	17 $-\ 8$	12 $-\ 5$	13 $-\ 7$	16 $-\ 7$	12 $-\ 4$	14 $-\ 7$

4.	10 $-\ 5$	13 $-\ 9$	14 $-\ 6$	17 $-\ 9$	14 $-\ 8$	11 $-\ 5$

Problem Solving *Reasonableness*

Circle your answer.

5. If Mary has 13 − 8 pennies and
   Terry has 13 − 6 pennies, then
   which sentence is true?

   Mary has more pennies than Terry.

   Terry has more pennies than Mary.

PROBLEM-SOLVING SKILL
Multiple-Step Problems

Solve each problem.

1. Jan read 14 books this month.
   6 books were about horses.
   The rest were mysteries.
   How many books were mysteries?

   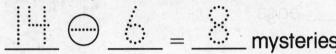

   14 ⊖ 6 = 8 mysteries

   Jan plans to read 4 more mysteries.
   How many mysteries will she have read in all?

   8 ⊕ 4 = 12 mysteries

---

2. Peter read 7 dinosaur books.
   He read 8 books about sharks.
   How many books did Peter read in all?

   _____ ◯ _____ = _____ books

   Of all the books he read,
   there were 6 that Peter didn't like.
   How many books did he like?

   _____ ◯ _____ = _____ books

Name _____

On the Farm

Solve.

1. There are 8 eggs in one nest.
   There are 7 eggs in another nest.
   How many eggs are there in all?

   _____◯_____ = _____ eggs

   Kendra is collecting the eggs.
   Her basket holds 10 eggs.
   How many eggs will be left in the nests?

   _____◯_____ = _____ eggs

2. There are 7 white hens. There are 5 brown hens.
   There are 3 hens that are gray.
   How many hens are there in all?

   _____ + _____ + _____ = _____ hens

3. Circle the strategy you used to solve Exercise 2.
   make a ten   use doubles

Writing in Math

4. Draw a picture of 13 eggs. Write a subtraction story about your
   picture. Then write a number sentence to go with your story.

   _____◯_____ = _____

Adding Groups of 10

Write each number sentence.

1.

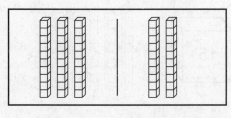

$\underline{30} + \underline{20} = \underline{50}$

2.

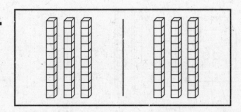

_____ + _____ = _____

3.

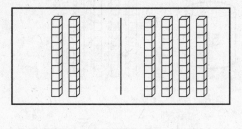

_____ + _____ = _____

4.

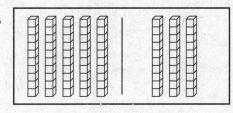

_____ + _____ = _____

Write each sum.

5. 50 + 20 = _____   30 + 40 = _____   20 + 20 = _____

6. 70 + 20 = _____   60 + 30 = _____   10 + 80 = _____

Problem Solving *Number Sense*

Circle the two groups that answer the riddle.

7. David has two books of stamps. He has more than
60 stamps. Which are David's stamp books?

Stamps of
the U.S.A.

40

Stamps of
France

20

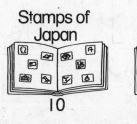

Stamps of
Japan

10

Stamps of
Mexico

30

Adding Tens to Two-Digit Numbers

Write each number sentence.

1.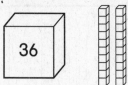

$\underline{36} + \underline{20} = \underline{56}$

2.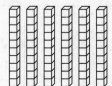

___ + ___ = ___

3.

___ + ___ = ___

4.

___ + ___ = ___

5.

63

___ + ___ = ___

6.

47

___ + ___ = ___

Problem Solving *Algebra*

7. Write the missing numbers. Then write the next addition problem in the pattern.

```
   37        47        57       [  ]      [  ]
 + 10      +[  ]     + 10      + 10      +[  ]
 [  ]        57       [  ]       77       [  ]
```

Name _____

Adding Two-Digit Numbers

Write each sum.

1.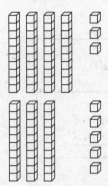

Tens	Ones
4	3
+ 3	5
7	8

2.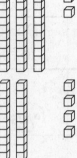

Tens	Ones
3	2
+ 2	4

3.

Tens	Ones
1	7
+ 6	1

Tens	Ones
6	3
+ 2	3

Tens	Ones
4	3
+ 5	2

Tens	Ones
5	3
+ 2	5

4.

Tens	Ones
3	5
+ 4	3

Tens	Ones
5	6
+ 3	1

Tens	Ones
4	3
+ 2	1

Tens	Ones
2	6
+ 2	2

Problem Solving *Reasoning*

Circle the number that solves each riddle.

5. I am less than 47 + 10.
I have fewer tens than ones.
Which number am I?

57   37   42

6. I am greater than 15 + 23.
I have more ones than tens.
Which number am I?

37   45   55

Regrouping in Addition

Use cubes and Workmat 4. Circle **yes** or **no**.
Then write the sum.

	Show	Add	Do you need to regroup?		Find the sum.
1.	27	6	(yes)	no	$27 + 6 = \underline{33}$
2.	43	5	yes	no	$43 + 5 = \underline{\hphantom{00}}$
3.	34	8	yes	no	$34 + 8 = \underline{\hphantom{00}}$
4.	17	4	yes	no	$17 + 4 = \underline{\hphantom{00}}$
5.	56	3	yes	no	$56 + 3 = \underline{\hphantom{00}}$
6.	93	2	yes	no	$93 + 2 = \underline{\hphantom{00}}$
7.	87	7	yes	no	$87 + 7 = \underline{\hphantom{00}}$
8.	68	5	yes	no	$68 + 5 = \underline{\hphantom{00}}$

Problem Solving *Number Sense*

Use the number line to add.

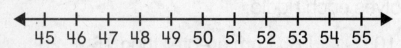

45 46 47 48 49 50 51 52 53 54 55

9. $47 + 6 = \underline{\hphantom{00}}$

10. $49 + 1 = \underline{\hphantom{00}}$

11. $46 + 3 = \underline{\hphantom{00}}$

12. $48 + 5 = \underline{\hphantom{00}}$

Name _____

Exact Answer or Estimate?

Circle **exact answer** or **estimate.**

1. Lizzie is making curtains.
   Each window is 36 inches wide.
   There are 2 windows.
   How much cloth should Lizzie buy?
   Do we need an exact answer or an estimate?

   exact answer   estimate

2. Don wants to buy peaches. They cost 50¢.
   Don has 2 quarters, a dime, and a nickel.
   Does he have enough money?
   Do we need an exact answer or an estimate?

   exact answer   estimate

3. Eric has 6 packs of trading cards.
   Each pack has 8 trading cards.
   He wants to give one trading card to each child in his class.
   There are 20 children in his class.
   Does he have enough cards?
   Do we need an exact answer or an estimate?

   exact answer   estimate

Problem Solving *Estimation*

Circle the better estimate.

4. About how many grapes
   can you eat?

   about 10   about 100

5. How many quarters can you
   hold in your hand?

   about 5   about 50

Subtracting Groups of 10

Write each number sentence.

1.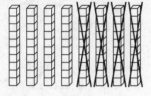

$$\dot{8}\dot{0} - \dot{4}\dot{0} = \dot{4}\dot{0}$$

2.

___ − ___ = ___

3.

___ − ___ = ___

4.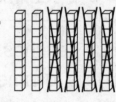

___ − ___ = ___

5.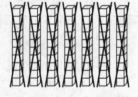

___ − ___ = ___

6.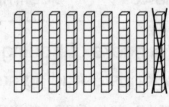

___ − ___ = ___

Problem Solving *Mental Math*

Solve.

7. Meg spends 70¢ on a pencil case and ruler.
The pencil case was 40¢.
How much did the ruler cost?

_____¢

Subtracting Tens from Two-Digit Numbers

Write each number sentence.

1.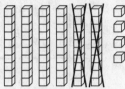

$$64 - 20 = 44$$

2.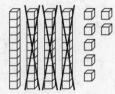

____ – ____ = ____

3.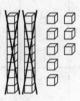

____ – ____ = ____

4.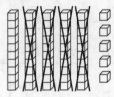

____ – ____ = ____

5.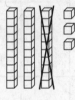

____ – ____ = ____

6.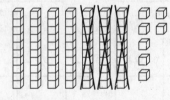

____ – ____ = ____

Problem Solving *Reasonableness*

7. Robert says that $75 - 30 = 35$.
Is he correct? Explain.

_____

_____

Subtracting Two-Digit Numbers

Write each difference.

1.

Tens	Ones
5	7
− 3	0
2	7

2.

Tens	Ones
4	8
− 2	4

3.

Tens	Ones
5	8
− 3	3

Tens	Ones
8	7
− 5	3

Tens	Ones
5	6
− 2	4

Tens	Ones
3	4
− 1	4

4.

Tens	Ones
7	5
− 4	3

Tens	Ones
6	4
− 2	2

Tens	Ones
3	2
− 3	2

Tens	Ones
9	6
− 5	4

Problem Solving *Algebra*

Write the missing numbers. Then write the next
subtraction sentence in the pattern.

5.

$$87 \qquad 77 \qquad 67 \qquad \square \qquad \square$$

$$-\,10 \qquad -\,\square \qquad -\,10 \qquad -\,10 \qquad -\,\square$$

$$\square \qquad 67 \qquad \square \qquad 47 \qquad \square$$

Regrouping in Subtraction

Use cubes and Workmat 4. Circle **yes** or **no**.
Then write the difference.

	Show	Subtract	Do you need to regroup?	Find the difference.
1.	42	6	(yes) no	$42 - 6 =$ 36
2.	37	5	yes no	$37 - 5 =$ _____
3.	62	4	yes no	$62 - 4 =$ _____
4.	58	9	yes no	$58 - 9 =$ _____
5.	24	7	yes no	$24 - 7 =$ _____
6.	77	6	yes no	$77 - 6 =$ _____
7.	85	8	yes no	$85 - 8 =$ _____
8.	93	3	yes no	$93 - 3 =$ _____

Problem Solving *Visual Thinking*

9. Draw the missing cubes.

Name _____

Make a Graph

Make a graph to solve the problem.
Color one box for every 10 books.

1. The first grade classes made a chart showing
   how many books they read each day.
   Which class read the most books?

Number of Books Read

Class	Day 1	Day 2	Day 3	Day 4	Day 5
Mrs. Miller's Class	30	20	10	10	30
Mr. Lee's Class	10	30	20	10	10
Miss Plum's Class	20	20	10	20	10

Mrs. Miller's Class										
Mr. Lee's Class										
Miss Plum's Class										

0   10   20   30   40   50   60   70   80   90   100

_____ class read the most books.

Writing in Math

2. Write another question that could
   be answered using the graph.

   _____

   _____

Caring for Kittens

1. Eduardo and his family went to the pet store.
   The pet store had 28 long-haired kittens and
   20 short-haired kittens. How many kittens did
   the pet store have altogether?

   _____ $\bigcirc$ _____ = _____ kittens

2. Eduardo gets a long-haired kitten.
   His sister, Elena, gets a short-haired kitten.
   How many kittens does the pet store have now?

   _____ $\bigcirc$ _____ = _____ kittens

3. Elena buys a toy mouse for her kitten.
   It costs 37¢. Elena has

   Will she get change? _____

Writing in Math

4. Eddie wants to buy a collar for 59¢ and a ball
   for 7¢. Does he need to regroup to find out
   how much they will cost? Explain.

   _____

   _____